The
BETTER
LEADERS
BETTER
SCHOOLS
Roadmap

small ideas that lead to **BIG IMPACT**

Praise for
The Better Leaders Better Schools Roadmap

Daniel Bauer's thinking about leadership, school, and life is long overdue in our profession—and it's like nothing you've ever seen. If you're looking for new energy, new ideas, and new inspiration, you'll find exactly what you need in *The Better Leaders Better Schools Roadmap*. Daniel's "small ideas that lead to big impact" reflect his wide reading, fresh thinking, and deep connections with innovative leaders across industries. Our schools will be immeasurably enriched through this book's impact on K–12 leaders.

Justin Baeder, PhD
author of *Now We're Talking! 21 Days to High-Performance Instructional Leadership* and director of The Principal Center, PrincipalCenter.com

Daniel does a great job of outlining the importance of school leaders to "think outside the lines." He gives the reader advice on how to look at their school with outsider eyes and take suggested tools to create a place where people are beating on the doors to get in. A quick and must read for the aspiring administrator and veteran school leader, alike.

John Fortney
BLBS Mastermind Member #1

Pure Meraki! In a social media-crazed-society that thrives on being "liked" and barely scratches the surface of substance, this book is the exact opposite, which is why you won't be able to put it down. Bravo, Danny!

Glenn Robbins
superintendent of schools for the Tabernacle School District in NJ

Danny Bauer's energy and enthusiasm lifted off the page! Bauer makes connections with our work as educators to one another. With many examples and strategies, Danny provides easy-to-follow advice on navigating through leadership for better schools!

Neil Gupta, EdD
director of secondary education

Danny's upbeat voice comes through loud and clear in this easy to read, supportive book full of strategies and tips for how to become a better leader. The text is straightforward, the author's voice is authentic and down to earth, and the ideas are truly useful. Thank you, Danny, for helping us once again to become better leaders for our schools and our systems.

Jennifer Abrams
consultant, speaker, and author of *Having Hard Conversations*

The Better Leaders Better Schools Roadmap is a powerful book. Written by one of the finest educational leaders I know, it is both a personal manifesto about what schools are for and a professional resource for anyone interested in becoming a better leader or improving the education profession. This unique book is well written and makes a compelling case not only for why we must make changes in our schools, but also what and how to change. It includes scores of practical resources for school leaders. Each chapter is an inspirational call to action that closes with specific and helpful "Next Steps" readers can take to make a difference in their own personal and professional growth as well as the students and colleagues they serve.

Jeffrey Zoul, EdD
author, speaker, leadership coach, and president of ConnectEDD

There's a reason people write manifestos, and *The Better Leaders Better Schools Roadmap* is an absolute throw down of what we all should be doing in our schools. Danny Bauer pulls on his almost two decades of experience as an educator and lays out the framework with a call to action for anyone working with kids. This book is a must-read, and I know will be a treasured gem for years to come!

Adam Welcome
author, speaker, educator, family, marathoner

This is a must-have roadmap for new and experienced leaders. The ideas shared, the resources provided, and the action steps at the end of each chapter equips leaders with the tools necessary to put their learning into practice. This resource is a game changer for leaders and schools.

Dr. Sanée Bell
principal, Houston, TX

With an honest and energetic voice, Danny "Sunshine" Bauer drives for the heart of the matter in educational change. The Better Leaders, Better Schools Roadmap lights up the soul of a leader in chapter after chapter with powerful queries and wholehearted encouragement while giving real-life strategies to advance a leader's practice. If you ache for more, you won't want to miss this manifesto for education and abundant toolkit for improvement.

Karine Veldhoen
school leader and author of
Learn Forward: An Invitation to the Most Important Journeys of a Child

Danny "Sunshine" Bauer is a master of developing positive attitudes in people that turns into personal success. Using his own personal experiences, along with the collective wisdom of world-class educators, he shapes an easy-to-follow plan to take action. *The Better Leaders Better Schools Roadmap* will help unlock your potential to be a great school leader.

Winston Y. Sakurai, EdD
2016 NASSP National Digital Principal,
2016 HASSA Hawaii Principal of the Year

Daniel Bauer is the real deal! He has been my mastermind mentor and coach for the last three years and has helped me grow both personally and professionally through his guidance, encouragement, and example. In his book, *The Better Leaders Better Schools Roadmap*, Daniel shares a wealth of knowledge and insight on how to grow and become the best version of yourself. Read it, apply it, and get ready to grow by leaps and bounds.

Nancy Alvarez
principal, #ECEchat co-founder, and owner of Teaching with Nancy, LLC

Danny is an inspirational leader who visibly walks the talk! His book, *The Better Leaders, Better Schools Roadmap*, will motivate you to get off of the couch, fill up your personal gas tank, set your GPS and take the journey that will improve your life and leadership skills.

Sandy King
instructional coach–Jordan School District and
recipient of Utah's Excellence in Education Award

Daniel Bauer is a leader worth following. I am thrilled that Daniel finally has the opportunity to put the brilliant ideas he shares online down into one book. This is a great book not only for school administrators but for all educators, for we all lead in one way or another. Daniel shares with heart but also with conviction. You'll definitely want to add this book to your collection.

Todd Nesloney
award-winning educator and principal,
best-selling author, and international speaker

Danny Bauer has been a leader of leaders for years with his successful podcast. Now with his book, *The Better Leaders Better Schools Roadmap*, you will be inspired while gaining practical tips to apply to your work today. Bauer's work is a compilation of some of the best resources and wisdom he has acquired from his conversations with a variety of exceptional leaders in the field.

Jessica Johnson
Wisconsin principal, author, and speaker

Rich, sensible, honest, and applicable insights, practices, and endless resources. This book is JAM PACKED with ways to develop your leadership. Through personal stories and an emphasis on accountability and collaboration, Danny provides the reader with useful and immediate solutions and advice for a plethora of leadership issues and healthy habits. It's a must-read and must-apply text!

Dr. Eileen Councill
deputy headmaster–curriculum & instruction, China

In *The Better Leaders Better Schools Roadmap*, Danny gives educators a clear road map toward success in schools as each section provides practical steps to engage in the work of leadership. He links relevant books, research, and voices from the field via his popular *Better Leader Better Schools* podcast so you can take the learning even further. From developing a culture to setting boundaries, Danny puts his heart and soul into each word—a must-read for all educators.

Jessica Cabeen
nationally distinguished principal,
author of *Hacking Early Learning*, co-author of *Balance Like a Pirate*

Entrepreneur and author Danny Bauer takes us on a pathway to the simple things that matter in education in his manifesto, *The Better Leaders Better Schools Roadmap*. Bauer shares his own personal experiences as an educator, a principal, and as an entrepreneur to remind us of the importance of focusing on the small, simple ideas that can make a lasting impact when it comes to not only improving schools but improving ourselves in the process. As a reader, I found his words and ideas sincere, authentic, refreshing, and most importantly, they served as a reminder of the responsibility we all have to lead for a better tomorrow for our students, staff, and schools.

Jimmy Casas
CEO, J Casas & Associates,
educator, author, speaker, leadership coach

Daniel Bauer's undeniable experience shines through as he initiates dialogue and sparks compelling conversations around the crucial questions of what is school for and what does it take to be an effective school leader. *The Better Leaders Better Schools Roadmap* is a book you'll want in your hands as it explores essential topics in education from a different angle and challenges conventional thinking. Providing practical tips, expert advice, and igniting unwavering inspiration to create the school of your dreams, this book serves as a game changer in education! Reading and joining in the conversations around the topics shared in *The Better Leaders Better Schools Roadmap* will propel you toward greatness as your leadership capacity increases as a result.

Elisabeth Bostwick
award-winning educator, author, and speaker

A must read for principals and aspiring leaders! *The Better Leaders Better Schools Roadmap* is exactly the kind of practical guide to school leadership needed in our educational system today. This book is high on my list of recommended reads.

D'Andre J. Weaver, PhD
husband, dad, school leader in Houston, TX

Danny Bauer shares from the heart. This book is a treasure chest of insights and practical strategies for school leaders learned through personal experience as well as through the years of research and interviews. Thank you, Danny, for taking time to share the valuable lessons you've learned and to do so with your authentic personality and voice.

Will Parker
host of the *Principal Matters Podcast*

You'll notice that the bulk of the Roadmap for a better school is focused on building yourself as a leader. Danny knows from experience how to be self-reflective and push himself to be the best. He distills these sometimes tricky ideas down to a level where you can take action. You don't have to be perfect, you just have to take action, every day, to make yourself better.

Jethro Jones
host of the *Transformative Principal Podcast*

The
BETTER
LEADERS
BETTER
SCHOOLS
Roadmap

small ideas that lead to **BIG IMPACT**

Daniel Bauer

The Better Leaders Better Schools Roadmap
© 2018 Daniel Bauer

Published by Better Leaders Better Schools

ISBN-13: 978-0-692-18525-4
ISBN-10: 0-692-18525-9

Edited by Jennifer Harshman, HarshmanServices.com
Cover and Book Design by James Woosley, FreeAgentPress.com

THIS BOOK IS DEDICATED TO A FEW IMPORTANT PEOPLE IN MY LIFE:

TO MY MOTHER, THERESA:
You have always believed in me and set the foundation that I could accomplish anything I set my mind to. Your example of hard work to provide for our family has paid tremendous dividends and thanks for helping behind-the-scenes as I built my company, BLBS.

TO MY AUNTS, DONNA & FLO:
You have also always believed in me and encouraged me from a young age into adulthood to pursue my dreams. We did it!

TO MY SISTER, CAROLYN:
Although I have plenty of podcast listeners and coaching clients, when you called and asked for leadership advice, my confidence in what I do soared to a new level.

TO MY BOYS, SILAS & LEVI:
You inspire me to make education better. When doing everything I do, I consider what kind of school experience I want you to have.

MOST IMPORTANTLY, TO MY WIFE, SHUPI:
What can I say? You are always there for me, supporting and loving me through the ups and downs of the entrepreneurial roller coaster.
I often say, "I couldn't do this without you,"
and you gently reply, "Yes, you could."
So what I mean to say is I wouldn't want to do this with anyone else.
You are everything I've ever wanted in a woman. I love you.

CONTENTS

Part Two: Changing Schools

FOREWORD

HAVING BEEN AN ENTREPRENEUR NOW for more than four decades has afforded me many personal and professional experiences. I've had the privilege to encounter various walks of life and literally had hundreds of employees in our previous fourteen businesses. So, I guess you could say I've been around the block.

Several years ago, I was introduced to a guy they called "Sunshine." Quite honestly, I admit that I thought to myself, "Oh, great. Here we go. Sunshine. Can't wait to see how this pans out." Well, nothing like I had anticipated, to tell you the truth. What was most important to me initially was the fact that he had a name, a real name. Daniel Bauer is one of the finest men I've met this decade. His care, compassion, and genuineness is contagious. His soft-spoken demeanor is coveted by many. His experience surpasses his age, and his sage wisdom is a force to be reckoned with.

When Danny told me he was considering writing *The Better Leaders Better Schools Roadmap,* I can't began to tell you my level of excitement. The truth of the matter is that we have a real void in education today with quality content and true and tested methods to educate my grandchildren and yours.

In this book, Danny does not shy away from the proven, tried-and-true principles nor is he bashful about introducing us to better options. Danny quickly dives into what the soul of a school leader looks like and why he is so passionate about what he believes. There are so many distractions today in the education system with all the bureaucracy devouring our precious time that we must educate ourselves both personally and professionally in order to best serve the recipient. Danny does not hold back for one second, as you turn the pages of this amazing resource.

Oftentimes, the basics are glossed over and set aside, and we feel that there is no real value in the human side of education. Danny is a master at demonstrating empathy and love, and he does not apologize for one instant in revealing the true essence of these virtues.

Well, I could go on and on revealing countless unmatched character traits and genuine leadership skills that Danny possesses, but time does not allow. I would suggest that you dive in for the ride of your life with a roadmap of sorts for how we can save the children and provide a sustainable way to better our education system.

If you want real value, you have found it in *The Better Leaders Better Schools Roadmap.*

Aaron Walker
View From The Top
president/founder

The Inspiration

In September of 2015, I set out to share my voice in education, and Better Leaders Better Schools (BLBS) was born. I started BLBS for a few reasons.

1. I wanted to have consistent, honest, and vulnerable conversations about school leadership. This was hard to do locally and regularly.
2. I was listening to a bunch of podcasts at the time and thought, *I could do that*, so I did.
3. I wanted to offer a great, free resource with high-level discussion around school leadership. Since then, over 100 episodes have been released and downloaded over 100,000 times.
4. In my humble opinion, thinking around education has become stale except for some pockets of greatness. I wanted to amplify the voices of leaders who are leading schools in courageous and innovative ways.

It has been an incredible joy and honor to create the BLBS blog and podcast for the world to interact with. It has opened many doors for me and pushed me out of my role as a daily practitioner to one of a thought leader and mentor of school leaders through masterminds. Now that I am running BLBS full time, I have autonomy over my schedule. Every minute I can spend intentionally while I work and focus on growing leaders. It has always been my goal to write a book for school leaders. I hope you find this product you are reading right now meaningful. Seth Godin inspired this manifesto after writing *Stop Stealing Dreams*. Seth's original work (plus many of the resources mentioned in the book) will be cited here and available for download on the book's website: BetterLeadersBetterSchools.com/roadmap. In Seth's manifesto *Stop Stealing Dreams*, he challenges the reader to rewrite, critique, and/or write their own manifesto. I chose the latter, and that is what is in your hands right now.

Building a Discussion

The purpose of this manifesto is to spark a dialogue and begin a conversation around a topic near and dear to my heart: education. I have been working in education since 2001, and I consider myself lucky. While many of my friends have fought through the rat race of corporate life and cursed every second of it to their friends, I have modestly earned a living while being blessed to wake up each day excited to go to work. It has been a pleasure making an impact on the future of our society.

In order to build a discussion, a medium and a platform must be provided. So consider this document the medium, and the platform can be found on Twitter. Just use the hashtag #BLBSRoadmap, and tag me (@alienearbud) in your tweet. I will respond to every tweet and cannot wait to see what you connect with in this book!

Essential to the success of this text and the following discussion is the concept of spreading ideas.

Additionally, I challenge you to write your own manifesto. Afterward, send it to me so I can forward it to my email list of education leaders and/or feature it on my blog (unless you turn it into a book, and in that case, send me the link to buy it!). Critique and challenge the content found here as well as write your own manifesto to share with the world.

Is that a scary idea? Probably . . . but the world will not benefit unless you share it . . . *and we need to hear from you*!

One of my favorite quotes comes from Derek Sivers: "What is ordinary to you is extraordinary to me."

You are the only one who can see the world as you see it. So good luck, and let me know when you have a finished product. Send your completed manifesto and/or link to the blog that hosts it to daniel@betterleadersbetterschools.com. I will share with the thousands of subscribers to my newsletter and share on social media. Education needs to hear our voices.

> ## A rising tide lifts all ships.
> —JFK

Introduction Resources

Seth Godin's original *Stop Stealing Dreams* can be found here:

- sethgodin.typepad.com/files/stop-stealing-dreams-print.pdf

One last reminder . . . all resources mentioned in the book will be available for download at:

- BetterLeadersBetterSchools.com/roadmap

PART ONE: LEADERSHIP

Soul of a School Leader

IN SETH'S MANIFESTO, HE EXPLORES two important questions that each education leader should explore for herself:

1. Why do we do what we do?
2. What is school for?

The remainder of this manifesto attempts to answer these questions broadly from a number of perspectives. Taking a look at these two questions is important for a variety of reasons. **"Why do we do what we do?"** reminds me of Simon Sinek's work and the idea of "starting with *Why*." This is similar to backward-mapping. The idea is that if we are clear on our destination, then we can reverse engineer or design a map to get us to the Promised Land.

Why matters more than most people realize. It is *the* motivating reason that inspires your staff. If the *why* is strong enough, people feel like what they do matters. The feeling of "What I do matters" is deeply significant. This leads to individuals thinking about change at scale— *Maybe my efforts can change not only my little corner of the neighborhood, but maybe, just maybe, the world, too.*

The second question is equally significant: **"What is school for?"** In my humble opinion, we have gotten wildly far from answering this question correctly in the USA. School seems to be more focused on test scores, funding, and political platforms. The world and technology are changing at an incredible rate. The jobs that existed just a decade ago are being replaced by computers, automation, and a global workforce that can do the job better and often cheaper. Yet school remains the same. The joy for learning has been slowly squeezed out of each school as US schools continue to produce compliant, linear thinkers who can answer multiple-choice assessments that are irrelevant in most other countries and day-to-day contexts.

What our students need now are training and mental models that foster independent critical thinking. Students need authentic learning experiences that revolve around projects and allow them to tinker and learn from their mistakes.

CHAPTER 1 NEXT STEPS

How would you answer these questions?:

- **Why do we do what we do?**

- **What is school for?**

I would love to hear how you might answer these two questions. Keep the conversation going on Twitter. Use the hashtag #BLBSRoadmap and share your thoughts. If you need more space, may I suggest composing an idea on your blog or a Google doc and share that with me (@alienearbud) via Twitter.

CHAPTER TWO

Hard Conversations

THE ABILITY TO HAVE HARD conversations is a hallmark of a great leader. Most people avoid them or blow them up after initially engaging. Great leaders lean in and deal with conflict in a compassionate, inquisitive, and direct way.

A few books that have really helped me understand hard conversations are these:

- *Having Hard Conversations*
- *Hard Conversations Unpacked*
- *Crucial Conversations*

It is much easier to avoid tough conversations. I avoided a tough conversation most of 2017 for two reasons:

1. I knew that I would not be staying at the school where I was working at the time. The writing was on the wall (I knew in October that I had to leave).

2. I did not see it as worth my energy to check in and challenge someone's toxic attitude. On my worst days, I feel like I copped out and avoided it because it was the easier thing to do. On better days, I realize that having the tough conversation was not worth my energy. The person I needed to talk to represented the unhappiest individual I have ever seen. Was I going to change that? Probably not. Maybe I should have tried. I have had crucial conversations in the past, though.

The best example I can think of was a tough conversation I held with two teachers who were treating each other unprofessionally. I evaluated them, and during closed-door meetings, they would tell me that everything was fine with the other. But then the team lead would also come visit my office to share some concerns.

"I can't take it!" Laura would exclaim, sitting defeated in my office chair. "I've tried everything, and they keep treating each other like children . . ."

So I called an off-site meeting at Starbucks. "What is this for?" the feuding teachers asked.

"I want to buy you both your favorite drink and have a conversation about how you can positively work together." I arranged with the attendance clerk to allow the teachers to come to school late and still get paid for a full day's work.

To my surprise, both teachers beat me to Starbucks, bought their drinks, and were having an amiable conversation. By the time I ordered a caramel latte and sat down, the relationship had already started to mend. From there, I just added the following ideas I have gleaned from the texts mentioned above.

1. It is important to assume the best intention of the other individual.
2. Start with the heart: Stay focused on what you really want.
3. You really can only control yourself . . . *How am I contributing to this situation?*
4. *What can I change and what is a healthy way to respond?*
5. Be observant. Look . . . people act differently (even weirdly) when they do not feel safe.
6. Find mutual purpose. Is there a shared goal that can be agreed on?
7. Commit to mutual respect.
8. Investigate the story I am telling myself and ask questions . . . *This is the story I am telling myself; can you correct where I am wrong?*
9. Question, listen, and reflect back to show active listening, engagement, and understanding.
10. Agree where possible.
11. Decide on a shared commitment moving forward.

Hard conversations are obviously difficult. If you find yourself (as I was) avoiding a conversation, send me an email, and I will encourage you to move forward!

Should-have Thinking

The most dangerous phrase in the English language is "should have." It is entitled thinking. Pity-party type of thinking. Whenever you find yourself thinking, *This should have . . .* or *This should not have . . .* **Stop!**

One idea that really challenged me in therapy was that everyone does not see the world the way I see it. What? Are you serious? I know! That should not have been such a shocker to me. This should be obvious to everyone, but I admit it was not apparent to me. Looking at any situation, I realized that some scenarios I have very strong convictions for. There is right and there is wrong, but not everyone may agree with my line of thinking. Line 10 people up in front of me, and chances are not only will they disagree with my sense of right and wrong, but they will disagree with each other, too. And that is okay.

I also found myself trapped in this type of thinking when considering the type of day I wanted to have. I had a type of plan and linear way of thinking about my day. When that plan started to veer off course, I became very irritable and a version of myself that I do not like. It could be as simple as wanting to drink coffee and have breakfast while I read in the morning. If anything (or anyone) interrupted that morning plan, then I would become frustrated. Negative. Pessimistic. I pointed fingers. It was everyone's fault except my own.

And what did I say to myself? *This day should have gone differently.* Or . . . *This experience should not have occurred this way.* Using "shoulds" and "should not haves" is like drinking poison. It is lethal. As a leader, eliminate this phrase from your mind. Replace it with getting curious and being flexible. The world is much more enjoyable when it is filled with wonder instead of "should-have" attitudes.

Wondering

If the word *should* is dangerous, then the word *wonder* is the antidote. I learned the phrase "I wonder if . . ." in 2014, when I was working at Brooks College Prep in Chicago, IL. My colleague Hector taught it to me and the rest of the staff, and I found the phrase extremely useful. It is now a go-to for me.

In education, just like anywhere else, we have to engage in tough conversations because the work is high-stakes. But often we remain silent or go into attack mode when conversations are difficult. The phrase "I wonder if" works because it is rooted in curiosity and is stated without judgment.

Wonderings help us converse about ideas and motivations. Wonderings help us be creative and find the best solutions.

Go ahead. Try it during your next tough conversation. Use it as a discussion starter. Have people write down their wonderings about a new policy, procedure, or expectation.

Dialogue will flow, and mutual purpose will be found because of the shared curiosity.

I wonder what might happen if we took this more humane and curious approach to debating difficult topics.

CHAPTER 2 NEXT STEPS

☐ Identify something that is frustrating. Are you playing the part of the victim? Are you suffering from "should-have" type of thinking? Get curious. Reflect. Apply the "magic" of wondering.

☐ Ask yourself growth-mindset questions:

- Be objective: What happened? What do I want? What are the facts?

- Take control: What choices do I have in front of me?

- It is important to become a learner instead of a judger.

- Recommended reading: *Change Your Questions, Change Your Life.*

CHAPTER THREE

The Team

Connection and Relationships

Building a platform to influence school leaders is no easy task. Leading a classroom, a grade level or department, a school, or a school district is also quite challenging. It becomes a whole lot easier when you connect with others.

Schools ask teachers to collaborate often, to pore over student data, personalize learning, and make choices that will benefit each student. Yet school leaders often work in isolation, facing challenging problems alone.

My friend Greg Salciccioli wrote a quick read and challenging leadership handbook called *Enemies of Excellence*. We read this text in my masterminds for school leaders, and everyone *loved* this book. The first enemy is isolation. When leaders work independently and operate as silos, they regularly make poor decisions. The only antidote is human connection.

Relationships are what make us stronger. It has been the counsel of close friends and colleagues that has helped challenge half-cooked ideas or helped good plans become great. This only happened when I invited others in.

> Alone we can do so little;
> together we can do so much.
>
> —HELEN KELLER

The default tendency to work alone is easy.

Sharing challenges and asking for help is scary.

Our ideas may have holes in them. Our actions may not be aligned with our values, and we may get called out for it. That is why relationships matter so much.

Today, relationships are easier to make than ever. Social media allows us to connect with others across the globe that a decade or two ago would have only been a sparse pen pal. I have friends literally on every continent, and I am better for it. When I take shallow relationships and engage deeply, the ROI on those relationships becomes even more profound. In the following graph, you can see that the quality of your connection with others is directly proportional to your level of awesomeness.

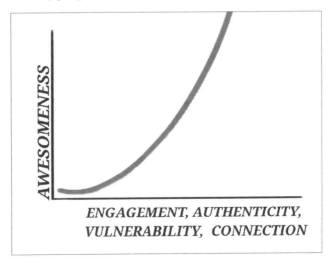

But not only does connecting matter, with *whom* you connect is also deeply important.

In the *NY Times* editorial piece, "Why Some Teams Are Smarter Than Others," the author explains three studies from MIT that looked at effective teamwork.

The findings:

- Smartest teams are distinguished by three characteristics:
    » Members contribute equally to discussion.
    » Members read emotions well.
    » Teams with more women outperformed teams with more men.
- This translated even to teams that worked predominantly in a virtual environment.

My key takeaways? Connecting matters. Diversity matters. (By the way, if we have not connected on social media, you can add me on all social media platforms. Links to everything are provided in the book's resources download at BetterLeadersBetterSchools.com/roadmap.)

> ## None of us is as smart as all of us.
> —KEN BLANCHARD

Team Strengths

There is a lot of talk concerning strengths and weaknesses. I side with the camp that thinks weaknesses should pretty much be ignored. Instead, we should focus on making our strengths our superpowers.

After all, if you are proficient in writing poetry but lousy at computer coding, why would you waste hundreds or thousands of hours trying to become a better coder? What if you really honed your writing craft and became the poetic voice of your generation?

In the introduction, I shared my favorite Derek Sivers quote: "What is ordinary to you is extraordinary to me."

Often, we take for granted what makes us special—the things that make us unique and extraordinary. That is a huge mistake.

We look in the mirror and notice only our faults.

A pimple here . . .

A wrinkle there . . .

A new patch of gray hairs that have sprouted . . .

Feedback does not help much, either. As students, we are trained to think in terms of weakness.

Turn in a paper. Here is your grade of 80. You lost 20 points from perfect because of these mistakes.

Fix the mistakes. Fix the mistakes. Fix the mistakes, and you will be better. Fix the mistakes to be top of the class. Fix the mistakes, and feel good for a few seconds, and never think of that perfect score again in your life.

Now look at the next weakness, and fix it. Keep fixing until you feel good.

Mistakes are exhausting.

Feedback from managers is not much better. Feedback to teachers is not much better. Focusing on problems, mistakes, and weaknesses cannot be the basis of feedback.

Dreams. Goals. Aspirations. Strengths. This is where we need to focus. Strengths.

What does your staff find inspiring? What do your students find inspiring? What do they like to do when no one is looking? Who are they as people, as individuals?

Get to know that. Get to know their strengths. Build upon them.

Now you are doing something great.

Building on strengths allows you to become something marvelous.

When you lead a project at your school, do you think with intentionality, *who has the skill set to really advance this idea?*

Or do you just plug and play?

You, yeah, you . . . I have a job for you (it does not matter what your skill set is).

Ways to Get Better Building on Strengths

Here are just two ways to get better at building on strengths.

1. Take StrengthsFinder 2.0 with your entire staff. Plot everybody's strengths. Think about what the data show and use that to inform your strategy and tactics. Here is the spreadsheet that I used at my former school to better understand my people.

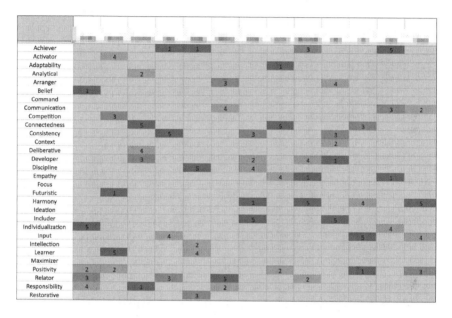

2. Use a DISC profile with your staff. The DISC personality profile is based on the work of Dr. William Moulton Marston, a psychologist who introduced the theory of these personality profiles in his text *Emotions of Normal People.*

Here is what DISC stands for:
- D = Dominant
- I = Influencing
- S = Stable
- C = Compliant

This is an interesting tool to use with your staff because it helps you understand their personality types and motivations. Each member of my school leader mastermind takes a DISC profile so I can understand them and so they can better understand themselves. The assessment tells you what motivates you, how you communicate, and how best to communicate with you—important info to share with colleagues! Here is how DISC personalities break down in terms of % of the population:

- D = 3%
- I = 11%
- S = 69%
- C = 17%

According to test results, 86% of the world's population is an S or C. Why is this important?

Because most leaders are D and I (14% of the population). Often our communication style defaults to what we like, which is a huge mistake. I am sure you have heard it said to "know your audience" when communicating. This data shows that leaders must adjust how they communicate so their message is received and understood by their people. A DISC assessment can help with that.

If you would like to order DISC assessments for your team, you can send me an email (daniel@betterleadersbetterschools.com). I can share a discount code with you, or you can order from the resources download available for this book. I sell DISC profiles individually and in bulk and would love to help you. I also can offer training for you and your staff (virtually) to help you better understand the power of a DISC assessment and its implications for your team. What would we cover in our training?

- History of the DISC profile
- Purpose of the DISC
- Each profiles strengths and fears
- Review your team's profiles
- Coaching session on how I would use the DISC with your team

Ask for Help

Greg Salciccioli taught me that the #1 Enemy of Excellence is isolation. If this is true, then a close second is a leader who keeps everything to herself. It is a myth that as the leader you need to do everything by yourself and/or have all the answers.

Great leaders confidently state when they do not have the answer and when they need help. Outside of a school getting help is easy: connect on social media or join one of my masterminds.

At the workplace, a leader just needs to ask people they trust and/or form a team that can handle the job at hand.

At Brooks, the leadership team realized we had been striking out regarding professional development (PD). We established an inspiring vision for where the school was moving and thought we knew how to get our staff there. However, we were moving forward while the staff was staying put.

The problem?

We were doing exactly to our teachers what we did not want them doing with our students. We offered one-size-fits-all PD without staff input. There was absolutely no personalization of PD, I am embarrassed to say.

The solution?

We formed a team of driven teachers to lead PD. We called it "PD@Brooks."

Teachers had to actually apply to participate on this team. If they were selected, we paid for an all-expenses-paid trip to a conference of their choosing. Five teachers were selected. They agreed that if they were chosen, they would share the information they learned from the conference as well as lead personalized PD sessions based on surveys of staff needs.

This never would have happened if we had not swallowed our pride and asked for help. The momentum gained from handing over the direction of PD to teachers never would have happened, either, if we had not asked for help!

Delegate. You Cannot Do It All.

You are just one person, and as much as your momma told you that you are Superman or Wonder Woman, you cannot do it all by yourself. There is a myth that has been told for centuries about leaders: **"Leadership is about being a superhero."** History books love to make ordinary men into superhumans lacking any real weaknesses. In the US, there is an idea of "pulling yourself up by your bootstraps." This mentality has inspired me and countless other leaders and entrepreneurs to be innovative and to take risks, but the danger is that it also inspires a cowboy mentality encouraging "going solo" rather than collaboration. No successful leader got there on her own. It was a team that helped her be successful.

The key to increasing your impact as a leader is to multiply yourself (and therefore your time) through other people on your team. You do this through intentional training, sharing of responsibilities, and smart delegation.

If you are anything like me, delegation may have been hard for two reasons:

1. You think you can do a task better than everyone else in the organization.
2. You find it hard to ask for help.

Even if you can do a task better than most (or all) in an organization, you should not necessarily do that task.

Why? Others on the team do not grow if you do not give them opportunities to learn and challenge their current skill set. Failure is a great teacher. If a teammate fails, this will provide an incredible learning opportunity for the individual. Given appropriate feedback, support, and training, this person will flourish under your leadership.

Also consider this: if another can do a given task at 80% the proficiency that you can complete a task, isn't that worth the time you will save? Like I stated above, the other person refines their skills while you have the opportunity to work on something more important.

If you find it hard to ask for help, just start, and start with people you consider "safe." People want to be a part of something bigger that is creating real change. This is the gift every school gives its employees: work that is inherently meaningful and beautiful. By asking for help, you include more people into the inspiring story of your school. If the work is meaningful, people will be happy to help out.

I teach a delegation roadmap in my *4 Steps to Better Leadership* course:

- the creation of an inspiring vision, mission, and values
- delegation roadmap
- powerful team meetings
- processes & systems
- goals that work
- organizational chart one-pager
- "magical" 3-in-1 job roles
- anxiety-free hiring
- and much more

In terms of the delegation roadmap, there are four to five rock-solid components, and I will share the most important idea here.

Write down every task that you are responsible for, and label each task as one that:

- gives you energy
- drains energy
- neither gives nor drains energy

Review your list. Keep all the tasks that give you energy, and delegate all the tasks that drain your energy (to the greatest extent possible). To go deeper with the delegation roadmap, you will have to enroll in the course, but powered even with that gem above, you can start delegating tasks better today.

Enough to Go Around

The world is connected, and we all benefit from sharing. The flip side is that no one benefits from keeping things to themselves.

Are you a "glass half full" or "glass half empty" type of guy or gal? Do you think there is enough to go around?

Personally, I believe in abundance and think there is enough to go around for everyone to be successful. However, others do not share this perspective.

They instead are filled with fear and pessimism. They think that by "sharing" (a skill taught to us in kindergarten), somehow they will suffer. I do not agree with that.

I encourage all the readers of this manifesto to share as much as they can around as many topics as possible:

- how to hire great people
- how to bounce back from a devastating loss at school
- how to inspire students and staff to greatness
- how to fundraise money and acquire grants
- how to use social media
- how to build a culture of restorative practices
- how to build student choice into the curriculum
- how to have hard conversations
- how to celebrate people
- how to get the most of connecting with other educators online
- etc. (what would you add?)

It is an honor to win awards such as Principal of the Year for your school to earn a fancy blue ribbon. These recognitions are important and validate your hard work, but they are extrinsic motivators, and deep down you need an engine that keeps you going within your soul.

In Chicago, the last school I worked at was considered selective enrollment. It was kind of like a magnet school, and students had to take a high-stakes exam to qualify, then rank, then wait to be selected by a selective school in the city.

The stakes were tremendously high. These were the best free schools that the city had to offer students. Some families felt as if there were no options for them and that their child was destined to a terrible life if they did not get into one of these schools (let alone one of the top selective schools).

Some families would take the test with integrity while others would lie, cheat, and steal to try to get accepted into a selective school.

The schools could be even worse. Rarely did anyone share strategies on how to attract the best students or what worked well for them during the recruitment phase. It was a cut-throat and competitive environment.

The biggest losers, however, were the students.

On top of all this, the (poor) communities were tragically under or misinformed about the process. As a result, a shocking number of qualified students missed out on a chance to attend a great school because they did not follow the appropriate admission guidelines.

I wonder what would have happened if we all pulled together. What would have happened if we shared the best strategies and got the greatest number of students into selective enrollment schools? Tragically, at the time, I did not have the correct mindset that I wish I had.

At that time, I did not know one can compete and still collaborate.

My mentor, Aaron Walker, used to own a highly successful construction company in Nashville, TN. Despite the wildly competitive environment, he would gather other construction company owners to collaborate, give/receive referrals, and share best practices.

The end result was that everyone had better information and could improve what they offered the community. Better homes were built for individuals and families. Better deals were made between contractors and suppliers of building materials. Everybody won.

Why does an abundance mentality work? What separates the good and great companies is execution. Everyone can have access to all the same information, but the winner executes the best and consistently provides great value.

There is enough to go around.

Share. Then execute.

CHAPTER 3 NEXT STEPS

☐ If the #1 Enemy of Excellence is isolation, then build your Professional Learning Network (PLN).

- **Novice Step:** Bring a local school leader (or two) out for coffee. Meet every month to check in.

- **Black Belt Step:** Engage on social media. Twitter and Voxer are popular hangouts for school leaders. Follow hashtags where the community is vibrant like #LeadUpChat, #KidsDeserveIt, #PIAChat, #EduGladiators

- **Jedi Step:** Join a mastermind I facilitate or start your own.

☐ Identify your team strengths with either a DISC survey or StrengthsFinder 2.0. If I can help in any way, let me know!

☐ List all the tasks you do in a given month. Identify what gives you energy, what takes energy away, and what neither gives nor drains you of energy. Delegate tasks that sap you of energy but give energy to others.

CHAPTER FOUR

Professional Development

People are Pegs

Treating people like pegs is an absolutely lousy way of running an organization. It is also the easiest and least inspiring way of running things. Have you ever heard the saying, "If the only tool you have is a hammer, everything looks like a nail"? Same idea here. Dangerous idea here.

It is kind of ironic, given the buzz around "personalization" in learning.

Yet regarding adults, "people are pegs" is the most common way of managing.

But managing is not leadership.

Leadership requires compassion, empathy, grace, patience, and understanding the individuality of staff members.

My friend D'Andre Weaver taught me lots about leadership and modeled it so well when we worked together at Brooks College Prep in Chicago, IL. One idea that he instituted (and that I admire) was a committee that handed over professional development to the teachers.

It was PD for the people, by the people.

This idea is echoed in *The Go-Giver Leader*, an amazing leadership tale by Bob Burg and John David Mann. The book teaches the principle, "The more you yield, the more power you have." I would rephrase this idea to **the more power you give away, the more power you have**.

And giving away power is exactly what D'Andre did —which made him that much more influential. By creating the committee stated above, teachers were resourced (e.g. attended conferences they were enthusiastic about) to pursue deep learning outside the school's walls.

There were three conditions to receive this money.

- Complete an application stating what you want to learn and why.
- Share your learning with the staff.
- Help build personalized learning for the staff during the school year.

By investing in teachers, D'Andre invested in the advancement of teaching and learning at Brooks.

It paid off.

People were pegs, but some were ovals, some squares, and even a few triangles. They were allowed to exist as the geometric shape God created them to be and the staff flourished as a result.

Deal with the humans who are in front of you. Not because it is easy, but because it is right and will lead to impact you can be proud of. Do not be a dam. Dams restrict the flow of water. Poor leaders restrict the flow of ideas. Do not be that kind of boss! To break out of the rut education finds itself in, we need to encourage bold, innovative thinking.

Teacher Committees

A teacher committee was formed to offer professional development by teachers, for teachers. Many administrators get caught up in the idea that "we know what is best" for our staff. To be honest, any leader worth her salt with an idea of how the school needs to grow, but without the support of the staff, the vision will never move forward.

Leaders talk about personalization and PD that can be used tomorrow in class. However, the reality it is much easier to plan "sit and get" PD . . . one size fits all.

This prioritizes the presenter and makes it easy for her while our people are disconnected, disillusioned, and uninspired to anything greater.

The fix . . . PD for teachers, by teachers.

At Brooks, teachers applied to form a committee (PD@Brooks). In the application they shared what their PD interests were and how they would give back to the community. When selected, these teachers went to a training anywhere in the US to learn a new strategy or skill to enrich their own instruction. In exchange for an all-expenses-paid development opportunity, they promised to share what they learned with the larger staff. Additionally, they would help plan personalized PD offerings to the staff for the entire school year.

By removing the admin from the process of PD@Brooks, we demolished a dam that had been stifling growth, innovation, and creativity. Leaders too often block ideas because of organizational hierarchy. If creative ideas cannot move forward without your stamp of approval, then give your stamp away to someone on the ground generating the ideas!

Focus on Success Rather than Achievement

When you get the opportunity to interview the Kansas Commissioner of Education, you shut up and listen to the wisdom (actually, I try to do that in every podcast interview, but this was a big moment for me).

My interview with Dr. Randy Watson (Bonus episode released April 2, 2018 on the BLBS podcast) included a number of gems, but the one that I really resonated with was the idea of forgetting about "student achievement" and focusing on "student success" instead. During the interview, Dr. Watson stated, "If we are only looking at test data and maybe some behavioral data during PLC times, we are truly missing the point of school. Students want and deserve so much more."

You see, Kansas has a bold vision: "To lead the world in the success of each student." What I love about this simple vision is that it is definitely a "moonshot" or, as Jim Collins would call it, a BHAG (Big Hairy Audacious Goal). When you cast the vision to lead the world, you are setting your sights incredibly high. And that is what vision is all about.

As a state leader, Dr. Watson led focus groups and re-presented the data he heard from them until he got a "that is right" answer from each group. By the way, that is a ninja-leadership lesson. Reflect back to anyone you are listening to until you hear "That's right." Once you hear that phrase, you have truly understood the other's point of view.

We should focus on success instead of achievement. You see, not every student is supposed to go to college. Shocking, I know! And when Dr. Watson listened to students, educators, parents, and the business community, they were in shocking agreement on one major issue: we focus too much on standardized tests!

In my opinion, the goal of NCLB was to raise the standard of instruction across the nation, but the flip side of this priority was putting less weight on (and in some districts, neglecting) all other aspects of the student development.

As a result, the arts, sports, and noncore courses got the shaft.

As a result, we did students a disservice regarding fully developing the whole child.

What does this have to do with professional development?

Everything!

It is a fine line to balance, but if you forget for one second that we are so much more than test scores and student-achievement data, you have missed the point entirely. We need to go all-in on developing "whole" human beings—the staff and our students.

If our PLC meeting and professional development focuses solely on test scores (standardized, formative, however you want to cut it), then I would argue we are not serving our kids at a high level. Standardized tests do not even measure intelligence that well. They do measure if we know how to play "the game" of school and testing. They do measure how compliant we are, and compliance is not a skill that will prepare the adults or children for the future.

So, what would I do?

Allow me a few questions you should at least consider. You are smart enough to design awesome PD around these questions, but if you could use some coaching, reach out to me via email at daniel@betterleadersbetterschools.com.

Questions to consider:

- How does my school prioritize wellness within my staff and students? How do we talk about it? How do we engage with wellness? Is it discussed during PD?
- Do you ever talk about the stress of being an educator and discuss healthy ways to manage the stress?
- How do we support mental and physical health at my school?
- In what ways do I recharge the batteries of my students and staff?
- Do we ever take time to dream about what school could be?
- Who is the student we want to produce after X amount of years under our care? Are we producing that kind of student? If not, where do we need to make adjustments? What kind of training needs to occur? What kind of courses need to be offered? How does the master schedule need to change? What kind of personnel do we need to add or repurpose?
- Who is the ideal staff member? Are we attracting that type of educator? If not, why not? What needs to change?

- How do we connect the passions of the community to the curriculum? Where do we need to make adjustments?
- Does the staff have an opportunity to be learners during the school year alongside the students? If not, how can the leadership encourage and incentivize learning?
- Have I investigated the Pareto Principle within my school? If 20% of what we do produces 80% of the results, that means we are collectively doing a lot of things that have little to no impact. What can be cut so we can go all-in on the 20% while running experiments of ideas that would bring more value to our community?
- Insert your interesting (non-student-achievement) question here.

Walking Among Gods and Goddesses

Attitude is everything. When I was a teenager, my mom bought me a shirt that said, "I love my attitude problem." I wore it proudly every chance I had. Too many of us wear a metaphorical "I love my attitude problem" to work every day. Our peers do not see the shirt, but they feel and experience the attitude. It is poisonous for the environment, and school leaders need to address attitude problems relentlessly, with compassion.

Some of our schools need to see an emotional chiropractor and get an adjustment.

How would your actions change if you thought your work occurred on sacred ground? One of my mastermind members and author of an amazing book, Karine Veldhoen, often shares that our work as school leaders and educators is sacred work.

Sacred.

Do we treat it as such? Sacred reminds me of the stories in the Bible where priests came upon holy ground. They removed their shoes for they dared not taint the sacred ground with their shoes. It was a sign of respect for a holy area. Schools are sacred. Do we treat them as such?

Another mastermind member, Fran McGreevy, loves to tell his staff that he is privileged to come into work every day (Search "Principal of the Year Retires with Epic Sendoff Message—Casey Middle School—Williamsville, NY" in YouTube to find the video or download my list of resources).

You know why?

Because according to Fran, each day he is "Walking among gods and goddesses." Fran is not all hot air, either. He backs up these encouraging words with actions that communicate that he cares. Whether it is writing thank-you cards, taking the time to be present and listen to a teacher's concerns, or removing obstacles and barriers in his staff's way of success, Fran communicates that he cares.

How would your actions change if you saw school as sacred and the staff as divine?

How far would your students go if your staff held the same opinion of their work?

You can listen to Karine's podcast episode and Fran's episode by downloading this book's resources.

CHAPTER 4 NEXT STEPS

☐ Form a committee where teachers own their PD. Empower them and watch the magic that follows.

☐ Run a PD that answers some of the questions stated in this chapter. If you do not know where to start, have the staff think about the kind of human being the school should help develop. Consider in what ways you are doing a great job of development and where you need to make adjustments.

☐ Make it challenging and ask "leaders" to give back to the staff. People want to live up to something meaningful, powerful, and bigger than themselves. People live for purpose. Provide them the opportunity to serve via a PD committee.

☐ Start seeing your community's work as sacred. If the school was built on sacred ground, how might that change your approach to the work?

CHAPTER FIVE

Healthy Self-Image

Are You (In)adequate?

The mirror is a scary place for me. It shows my blemishes and the warped sense of way that I view myself from time to time. Many times in front of the mirror, I prayed that I view myself as God views me. I cannot state how important that prayer was for me in my life.

Other tools I have used to battle a negative view of myself include: therapy, a mindfulness meditation practice, and journaling.

The combo of spirituality + therapy + meditation + journaling has led to a life where I viewed myself realistically and became more emotionally healthy.

A healthy self-image is a prerequisite for greatness and accomplishing your dreams. You absolutely cannot accomplish anything meaningful with an inadequate view of yourself plaguing you.

Seeing yourself in a negative light is creating a ceiling about two inches above your head.

It creates an upper limit in terms of thinking and accomplishment. This barrier must be removed in order to achieve great success. To create and maintain a healthy self-image, I suggest a few things:

Spirituality

Connecting with a higher power has had great influence on me. I feel less alone and feel like there is a good plan for my life. Believing that all people were created in God's image cannot help but make you feel great and influence how you see and interact with people.

Therapy

Everyone has issues. Some people bury them, and others work through them. I choose to be a part of the latter camp. By exploring and gaining strategies to deal with issues, my demons pop up less and less in my life (especially at inopportune times), and I can navigate each day in a much healthier way.

Meditation

Mindfulness meditation has helped increase my awareness of what is going in my heart, my head, and my body. Why is this important? By "tuning in" to these places, I notice what is going on and explore why that is. By noticing, I also am less likely to be influenced (negatively) and make poor decisions because of what is happening inside of me.

I like this description of meditation. There is a calm lake. The water is beautiful, crystal clear, and you can gaze all the way to the bottom of the lake. Then a storm comes in . . . waves start to crash, mud is kicked up from the bottom of the lake, and the water becomes murky. This is what happens naturally in life with its trials and tribulations. Through meditation and focusing on the breath, I am able to shoo away the storm and return the lake's water (in my mind) to a calm place where I can again see to the bottom. It is peaceful at this lake.

I highly recommend the Headspace app, Calm, or my current favorite, Oak.

Gratitude Journal

Your attitude dictates everything. At the end of every podcast, I share this quote:

"Remember that life is 10% of what happens to you and 90% of how you react to it."

I also have shared many times on the podcast about the power of changing your attitude into one that is more grateful. The main way I have done this is through a gratitude journal. I have talked about this routine on Episode 90 on the podcast. Here is how you set it up (and it literally takes five minutes) . . .

MORNING

- ☐ What am I grateful for today? (Write three things)
- ☐ What would make today great? (Write three things)
- ☐ Daily Affirmation (I am _____).

EVENING

- ☐ What amazing things happened today? (Write three things.)
- ☐ What could I have changed to make today better? (Write one thing.)

If you do this consistently day after day, you will develop a positive attitude made of steel.

Recently, I changed my journaling format. Now I divide a sheet of paper into six equal boxes and I answer these questions:

1. What could I have changed (yesterday) to make the day better?
2. What am I grateful for? (I can list as many as I want.)
3. What would make today great? What is my plan? (I list as many as I want.)
4. How can I help someone else today (and not expect anything in return)?

5. Notes from what I read this morning:
6. Open space . . . I can doodle, journal, or do whatever I want
    in this box (I can even leave it blank!).

You can see a picture of this new journal format by downloading the book's resources.

Affirmations

Each morning, I get up and say my affirmations. The short and sweet affirmation I recite is: "I am a success. Nothing can stop me. I have a plan that I execute every day. I trust the process. The results will follow. Love is at the center of what I do. I am here to serve. Generosity gives me great pleasure. I am living an optimal life that is satisfying." The longer version is available in my book's resource page. I learned about affirmations first from *Over the Top* by Zig Ziglar. He recommends writing on a 3 x 5 card and reciting every day. I next heard about affirmations from Hal Elrod via *The Miracle Morning*.

Both of these men have been extremely successful. If they say affirmations are important, then I believe 'em! Affirmations are important because they are reminders of our inner greatness. They should be written accurately, but they may include aspirational goals as well.

Visualization

Hal Elrod also taught me the power of visualization. The power of visualization is to positively frame your day . . . to actually see yourself as a success before you even attempt the tasks in front of you. It is like you are doing positive mental practice before arriving at whatever event will meet you that day.

My high school swim coach taught me visualization before a sectionals meet. He had me visualize the entire event. I visualized everything from the preswim activities (e.g., stretching, walking to the swimming block, putting the goggles on, etc.) to the actual race (how I entered the water, how long each stroke was, where I took my breaths, how I stretched to win the race, etc.) to the race finish (looking into the crowd, pumping my fist with excitement after the win, etc.).

Visualization is powerful because you are telling yourself you will be successful before you even make an attempt. Of course this needs to accompany hours of practice, but in addition to the blood, sweat, and tears you put into your work, visualization helps positively frame your mind for success.

Intentionality with Time (Do Things That Make You Feel Good)

How you use your time is incredibly important. We often go through life haphazardly without a plan. A fire starts; we put it out. An "urgent" email pings us; we answer it. Then at the end of the day, we look back and realize we accomplished pretty much nothing.

And that is just in our professional lives.

Living without intention also impacts us personally. If we are not careful, we rob ourselves from the joy of life because we do not make time to engage in life-giving activities.

I use a tool called "The Ideal Week" to plan out each week, and I make sure that I leave time to connect with my family as well as schedule time to do the things I enjoy. That way, I know fun is embedded into each day, and I can look forward to when that time will occur!

If you focus on the strategies above, you will help flip any "stinkin' thinkin'" you may have developed and take an inadequate view of yourself and changed into an adequate one.

Now go conquer the world!

Mindfulness and Meditation

Mindfulness. Meditation. You may have been hearing a lot about these topics lately (or at least I have). That is because these practices have greatly impacted my life. I also attribute it to that thing that happens when you buy a new car. Thanks to your Reticular Activating System, sometimes referred to as your RAS, after you buy a Honda Accord, you see a Honda Accord everywhere. At the grocery store, on the highway, etc.

I have always been interested in mindfulness and meditation. These are two distinct terms that I would define as follows.

Mindfulness: The process of noticing what is happening without judgment. It helps you grow in awareness of what is going on and aids in being present in a given situation.

Meditation: In my practice, meditation means that I focus on my breath and attempt to empty my mind. It is a single point of meditation. It is meant to add more peace and joy to my life.

Both practices put together offer me a way to "reset" within a day. An illustration I learned from the app Headspace helped me understand why these practices are so important. Imagine a serene lake anywhere . . . like the one pictured below.

This is our mind. Before the pressures of the day hit us, the water is calm and crystal clear. Looking deep into the water, we notice that we can see all the way to the bottom of the lake. It is peaceful.

As the day progresses, different stressors occur, which we handle in a variety of ways. Those stressors are like a storm; the rain beats on the lake's waters. The mud and sediment from the bottom of the lake get kicked up and the wind blows fiercely, causing great waves to ripple across the surface of the lake. The calm and serene setting is now one of chaos, and we can no longer peer into the bottom of the lake.

Mindfulness lets us pause during this storm. It encourages us to notice the storm and what has caused it. As we focus on the breath, the storm eventually fades. Not by our own effort but by our focus on the breath and our noticing of the storm without judgment. The waves die down, and the mud returns to the bottom of the lake.

The water is calm again, and we can see to the bottom of the lake. Peace, contentment, and joy have returned to us. This is the power of a mindfulness and meditation practice. This is what it has done for me.

Meditate

My life can be hectic. If I do not intentionally slow down, I run from task to task, meeting to meeting, at a frenetic pace. My heart pumps, "Full speed ahead!" and before I know it, the day is over. Mentally and emotionally, I am a mess and wound up as tight as a jack-in-the-box waiting to explode!

The demands of a school leader are many. In my opinion, a key skill a leader must learn is how to navigate the deluge of information, questions, and choices thrown at him in a day. According to various internet sources, leaders make an estimated 35,000 decisions each day! So what is a leader to do?

I think strategies like prioritization, delegation, automation, etc. are key to your success. In *Procrastination on Purpose*, Rory Vaden presents the "Focus Funnel," which is an important mental model for leaders to use in dealing with the 35,000 decisions waiting for them each day

In addition to these helpful mental models, I challenge leaders to take short breaks within the day to focus on their mental health through mindfulness and meditation. During an ideal week, I take a 10-minute meditation break before or after lunch.

My preferred method is to use an app like *Headspace* because I like how it teaches me to meditate. I have also used *Calm* and *10% Happier*. All are good options and have a free version. I encourage you to test them all out and stick with the one you connect with most.

When I take time to meditate, my mind and emotions are able to settle. Meditation also allows me to increase my focus, enjoy the day more through being present, and offer my best version of myself to the world.

If I miss meditation, I find that I am more impulsive, impatient, and a relatively rotten scoundrel. If I find time to meditate, I am more patient, compassionate, generous, and just a better human.

Personally, I shoot for 10 minutes using the *Headspace* app, but if that sounds like too much time, then just go for 5 minutes—even 1 minute!

If you cannot find time to meditate for 1 minute . . . well, you have bigger problems, and meditation will not fix those!

One book that I suggest all readers explore is *Search Inside Yourself* by Chade Meng Tan. We read this in the mastermind. Clients loved the text because it gave a scientific and secular view on how to practice mindfulness and shared data presenting the scientific benefits of mindfulness.

A few other resources you may enjoy are my friend Bruce Langford's podcast, *Mindfulness Mode*, as well as Dan Harris's *10% Happier* podcast. I believe if school leaders were able to steal just 10 minutes a day—perhaps after lunch—to hit the reset button, our schools would benefit immensely. Our lives can be stressful, chaotic at times. How much more could you serve your community if you were at ease and calm when facing the day-to-day needs of your community?

CHAPTER 5 NEXT STEPS

☐ Start a "Miracle Morning Practice," and start small. You can begin with just six minutes a day when you go through each step. Personally, I have graduated to an hour of this time + an hour to work out. When I was a building principal, I worked out for an hour and spent 30 minutes on the other steps.

☐ If "The Miracle Morning" seems like a lot to bite off at one time, start small. What one activity would give you the most benefit?

☐ Consider what your soul needs to be recharged. Would you benefit from some time in solitude, a massage, a hike in the mountains, or a session with a therapist?

CHAPTER SIX

Connecting and Masterminding

Connecting for Others' Benefit

My mentor, Aaron Walker, recently challenged the group of men he coaches to connect two people that could benefit each other—no strings attached. Too often we think, *What is in it for me?* Like gratitude, generosity is a skill that I have to consciously work on to develop and make a more natural part of my character. It reflects who I want to be, so I make it a priority. My experience in education has been an isolating one.

Change is hard, and the status quo continues without challenge if we work on our own. Not only do we benefit from connection, but we grow. And that means at the end of the day, our students and communities benefit. We become better leaders when we are connected leaders.

I do not have all the answers. I do not want to be the smartest guy in the room. If I am the smartest guy in the room, I am in the wrong room!

I am a learner through and through and thrive on asking questions and learning from others. It makes me better.

Aaron Walker's challenge was enjoyable. I experienced huge benefits and enjoyed the process of deeply thinking about who would benefit from being connected.

Now, I challenge you: Who do you know that is an excellent communicator or culture builder? Who do you know that is wise beyond their years? Who would benefit from being connected?

In this exercise, you do not have to facilitate where the conversation goes or if a relationship develops. You merely have to create the connection.

Goals

The easiest way to accomplish nothing is by drifting through life. Without goals, there is a lack of focus, and although you are certain to accomplish something every day, I guarantee you will not be thrilled with the results.

Back in March 2016, I went to my first mastermind meet-up with my mentor and fellow masterminders at View from the Top with Aaron Walker. We spent 2.5 days at a ranch in the Middle-of-Nowhere, Texas, 1.5 hours outside of Dallas. It was a beautiful ranch and a milestone event in my life. Because of this community, I have multiplied my goals by 10x and have accomplished so much more than I thought I was capable of. The keys to success are community and accountability. These components help you set bigger and better goals to crush.

Around the same time, I was finishing up Michael Hyatt's book, *Living Forward*, a book on life planning. Reading this book plus regular participation in my mastermind is like a punch in the face (in a good way).

Hyatt's book walked me through the steps of creating a life plan through an incredibly detailed process. I share this method and teach much more in my #GoalCrushers Group Coaching.

March 2016 . . . I had a very modest goal: start one mastermind for school leaders. I saw the power it had in my life, and I noticed a huge void of authentic connection for school leaders. So I filled that gap with my mastermind program for school leaders. In May of 2017, I updated my life plan and had to laugh at the goal because I have absolutely crushed it.

Mastermind Timeline

March 2016: Goal set and first mastermind launches (six clients)

July 2016: Second mastermind opens (13 total clients).

August 2016–March 2017: No attempt to grow mastermind and focusing on being a principal

April 2017: Focus on growing masterminds. Open third mastermind.

May 2017: Double the size of mastermind clients to serve (26 total clients). Close mastermind because of time capacity.

July 2017: Reopen masterminds since I am pursuing BLBS full time . . . In April and May of 2017, I doubled the size of the mastermind. It took some hard work, but the real reason I was successful was that I had a very focused goal, a system to execute on the goal, and a group of friends to encourage me and challenge me to execute. I now teach this method in my #GoalCrusher six-week coaching course.

If you take this course, I guarantee you will accomplish more in 12 weeks than most people do in 12 months. Click here for the details.

My clients have been incredibly successful and thoroughly enjoyed the course. I can teach you to get more done using my proven system. Check out this free webinar to get a taste of what we will discuss.

The Power of Community

In his excellent book, *The Enemies of Excellence*, Greg Salciccioli explains how **isolation** is the first pitfall that leaders must face in order to avoid disaster. When I started BLBS, I wanted to grow as a leader. I was facing my first role as an AP and I wanted to *accelerate my leadership development* through authentic, deep, and vulnerable discussions around this topic. I wanted to learn from people who had more experience. Learn from their wins but also from their losses. There is a lot of wisdom gained in our failures! Unfortunately, getting together locally and consistently proved to be very difficult. Ironically, when I decided to start a podcast and talk to leaders across the globe, the conversation I was seeking to have was also *easier* to have! I became a little more connected. Around the same time I started the podcast, I also joined Aaron Walker's Iron Sharpens Iron mastermind. We met weekly, and at the time it cost members $350/month. Ouch! I had never invested that much in myself before.

But it was worth it.

In just a few months, I was growing by leaps and bounds both personally and professionally. The men in the group helped me chip away at my ego and other unwanted character flaws. They helped me grow the BLBS podcast and start two online businesses. My mastermind helped me through a divorce. These men helped me push forward through the shame of being forced to resign from leading a school.

The biggest takeaway from that experience is yes, it was politics. And what I learned from that situation is when you play politics and someone bigger than you is on the playground, they might bully you until you leave.

That was one of the hardest experiences of my life. The mastermind helped me through it.

The mastermind also helped me value challenges and obstacles— even when they are unwarranted. Through each difficult situation, I came out on top.

After a divorce, I met someone that literally is my dream girl in real life.

After being pushed out of a principal position, I grew my coaching business and now get to serve an international group of leaders on a weekly basis. My work is filled with meaning, value, importance, and purpose. My impact grew exponentially, too, from 1,500 kids to 39,000.

I will take 12 rounds in the ring with a bully any day of the week if I come out like that!

I am currently the best version of myself, and that confidence, self-awareness, and success can be directly linked to the mastermind.

That's because Jim Rohn's quote is correct: "You are the average of the five people you spend the most time with."

The first time I heard that quote, I was absolutely *wrecked*. Where was I going? Did the community I invested in help me get there or hold me back?

Now insert the context of leadership (often done in isolation).

It is my goal to battle the isolation that plagues school leadership and transform the face of education across the globe.

The good news . . . It is happening:

- Karine raised 1.5 million dollars to save her school.
- Fran and Suzanne won Principal of the Year for their district; Jessica won this distinction for the entire state of Minnesota.
- Then, Colin won Charter School Principal of the Year in New Jersey.
- Jason and Nancy accepted their first principal roles (by the way, Jason found out he was interim principal one week before starting and then successfully was chosen to become the contracted principal after the district concluded its interview process).
- We helped Robert, Sam, and Fred throughout their first year as principal; Karla became a district science lead in Montana for more schools than I can count.
- Everyone was helped through countless personal and professional challenges, too many to list here.

In addition to the life transformation you will experience, when you join the mastermind, you instantly plug into a group of driven and hungry leaders. You absolutely upgrade your relationships as many of the members will become close friends and confidants. You are welcome to join the party!

I talk about the mastermind on my podcast. There is information about it on my website and the resource page for this book. You can also email me at daniel@betterleadersbetterschools.com for more information.

Visit Other Schools

One of the best ways to improve your school leadership is to learn from others. We have talked about the power of connecting online through social channels and the value of finding your voice through a blog, vlog, or podcast. Another great way to "sharpen your saw" is to improve and increase your network through school visits.

Ask to visit the school that is down the street and has a reputation of high achievement. Ask to see what makes them great. Build relationships. Steal and apply their ideas. We do not need to keep best practices to ourselves. What is the point in that?

Visiting other schools always did three things for me:

- It connected me to other great leaders.
- It inspired me and taught me new strategy.
- It emboldened me (We are currently doing it better or I think we can do it even better)!

These days, it is even easier than ever to connect with other leaders. Clients in the mastermind have actually traveled to visit each other's schools—to see a friend and to learn!

Want to go above and beyond the rest? Want to get your foot in the door of an awesome school? Make a personalized video for the leader of the building you are trying to connect with using a free service like Loom or an even better paid-for service like Bomb Bomb.

Tell them what you appreciate and what you admire about their school. If they create content (e.g. podcast or blog) respond to a recent piece. And then share something about yourself.

Keep it short, somewhere two to three minutes in length. Boom. You are in. If they do not respond to this, you probably do not want to work with that person anyway because you are focused on connecting using modern and efficient methods.

Be Authentic
AUTHENTICITY PART I: THE SELF

> Authenticity is a collection of choices that we have to make every day. It is about the choice to show up and be real. The choice to be honest. The choice to let our true selves be seen.
>
> —BRENÉ BROWN

Who are you? This is an important question to answer for any human being. It does not matter if you are a leader or not. Who are you, and how do you even know who you are? When I was a novice teacher, I remember idolizing this 8th grade Social Studies teacher. He was able to get his class to stand absolutely silent in a straight line before entering his class . . . every day and every single class period.

So I tried it . . . and failed miserably.

You see, this guy was a former military man. Me? Not so much.

My classroom has always been an example of controlled chaos. I love discussion, Socratic Seminars, students wrestling with problems and projects and getting frustrated when the answer seems difficult.

My go-to phrase as teacher was "Hmm . . . I do not know. How would you solve this problem?" I played music that students liked. I happily let them "own" the room and their learning.

Worksheets rarely made it into my class, and I only used rows of seats if I had to. I happily gave away power to the students every year (and then teachers as a principal) because my personality does not mesh with being authoritarian. I do not like being led that way, and I refuse to lead that way.

When I tried to be the 8th grade science teacher, I was being inauthentic to my true self. The kids knew it, and they revolted. They started a coup and toppled the doppelgänger dictator I had become (for a few days). Then things were back to normal.

It is dangerous to be somebody we are not. It is dangerous because we are robbing the communities we serve from the true gift that we are. Whatever makes us special and unique is worth sharing with the world.

People crave authenticity.

Kids and adults can smell a rat . . . a faker . . . a mile away. If you are faking because you are insecure or faking because you have an evil agenda, both are dangerous because they erode trust—the foundation of any high functioning team and organization.

No matter how scary or challenging it may be, show up as the real you. Every day. Then do it again. And again.

Yes, you might get rejected, but I would rather be rejected no matter how painful that is than be tolerated as a shadow version of myself.

It is freeing to give yourself permission to be yourself.

It is time to show up. Your community needs you. Let yourself be seen.

AUTHENTICITY PART II: THE WORK

If becoming an authentic version of yourself is instrumental to your impact . . . if authenticity is pivotal to true contentment in life . . . then authenticity with your work is the next most important step. Showing up as your true self is a gift to yourself and others. So is doing the work that matters each and every day.

When I was a kid, I had big dreams. Slowly, as the days passed, those dreams became smaller and smaller. The dreams also became safer and safer.

At one point, I woke up and yelled, "Enough!"

Well, I did not really yell to myself, but I made a conscious choice in the deep realms of my soul to show up as the real me and only do work I found meaningful.

What is life if we are not pursuing our dreams and trying to make the exact impact we want to make in the world? What is life if we are merely "playing it safe" and "doing what we are told"?

Forget that! Life is too short for merely complying.

From now on, I commit to following my dreams and doing bold things. I commit to the idea of "carpe diem" that I took inspiration from as a youth in high school and then forgot about as an adult. Swing for the fences. You are either going to strike out (and learn and get better and be proud for having stepped up to the plate) . . . or you are going to make *contact* and hit a home run, maybe even a grand slam, and really make an *impact*.

Do work that matters. Do it in public. Make a difference. Be memorable.

I admire Seth Godin for a number of reasons, but mainly because he has inspired me:

1. Do work that matters in public.
2. Ship it before it is perfect. You can always change it and improve it later.
3. Seth has also taught me how to care deeply about others and think about how best to serve them.
4. Treat my work as a form of art.

I admire Steven Pressfield because he put language around that terrible voice inside all our heads. Steven calls it "*The Resistance.*" That is the voice that tells you the idea does not matter, or that no one is paying attention to what you create, or that you are plain ole' stupid.

The Resistance attempts to shut you down before you even get going, but you can learn to defeat The Resistance.

Finally, I admire Jennifer Abrams. We have connected a number of times on the podcast (EP 036 and EP 088). She has inspired me and challenged my thinking in so many ways. I do not have any idea how to repay her! In 2017, we started talking about how to best make an impact in the world, and she came up with the idea and phrase, "playing in the deep end." This is now a personal mantra of mine. To me, it means show up every day and take risk.

It is worth it. The shallow end is safe (and not very fun). Sure, I may drown if I go to where my toes do not touch the bottom, but it is in the deep end where I get stronger. The deep end teaches me to trust myself. Here, I look fear in the eye and when I survive, I am a much better person.

Do not lie. Isn't this obvious? As a leader, your character and integrity . . . your word is everything. People are watching you from every angle including what you say and do online. Be honest and do not lie.

Sometimes in relationships, I have bent the truth. I have done that because of fear. I was scared of the implications of the truth. *Will my partner leave me if she knew this about me?*

That is my insecurity. I do not have any major crazy secrets to hide, but whatever demons I do wrestle with, they tend to grow into monsters in the dark. When it is just me and my thoughts (especially about my imperfections and what I am not proud of), they grow and grow until they are as big as Lord Voldemort or Lord Vader proportions (note to self . . . do not name a kid with the letter V . . . they will turn rotten).

And then I bend the truth because I am scared and insecure.

Candor is freedom. When you share about yourself, offer an opinion about someone's performance, or have to decline an invitation, by sharing honestly, you say to the other individual, "I trust you with this information." If you are like me and sometimes withhold information because you are scared, you rob someone of the ability to act with compassion and grace. For some reason, this is not a problem for me at work, but personally it can be.

Many characteristics matter in a leadership position, and honesty is at the top of the list. Do not lie on evaluations because it is easier to push someone out. Do not lie about what you have or have not done to save face in front of colleagues or your boss. Fess up and be honest. There is respect in the moment truth is shared even when it is not pleasant. Trust erodes when one finds out that you were dishonest. And trust is the foundation to great organizations. You accomplish nothing that lasts without trust.

CHAPTER 6 NEXT STEPS

☐ Make a life plan (read Hyatt's *Living Forward*) or invest in my productivity course, where I will teach it to you as a bonus. Of course, you can do the research yourself and do it as well, but the idea is simple: live with purpose!

☐ Get connected. Expand your PLN, attend conferences, and join my mastermind, or start your own.

☐ Blog, vlog, or podcast. Your self-awareness and voice will be supercharged if you regularly communicate what you are all about.

☐ Visit a school to learn how other people are running great schools. This can be easily done within your district or be adventurous and reach out to a school leader you admire and ask to visit her school.

CHAPTER SEVEN

Self-Development

Meet-ups and Are You Developing Yourself?

As a recovering introvert, I have spent a lot of time by myself. I honestly avoided crowds whenever I could. Some people have mistakenly thought I was a practicing monk for how much I enjoy solitude.

There is absolutely nothing wrong with being an introvert, but interestingly, once I started a podcast, I saw my personality begin to change. That kind of happens when you start talking to strangers on a regular basis! Probably 20–30 episodes in, I really started getting comfortable. People said, "Danny, you make it really easy to talk to you." That unlocked something inside my head where I wanted to start talking to more people (even outside of the podcast).

Luckily for me, I did. Since I started pursuing more conversations and investing in more relationships, I have grown tremendously. The diversity of opinions and ideas that I am exposed to on a regular basis pushes my thinking and helps clarify the vision of where I am going both personally and professionally. It also helps me hone and amplify my voice so that my message is clear to the world.

If you are not yet at the step of engaging with people regularly, then I humbly suggest that you read widely and consistently. You can do the same by listening to podcasts. By exposing yourself to the diversity of ideas out there, you will be forced to grow. Of course, you must objectively evaluate each idea as it comes in and try to avoid any cognitive bias that may exist.

The next professional step would be to start going to meet-ups that interest you. In the sphere of education, nothing could be better than an ed camp. First, it is free, so it will only cost you in terms of time and how you arrange to transport yourself there. Second, you will surround yourself with new people and ideas, benefiting from the improvisational professional development of an ed camp.

After an ed camp, look for local meet-up groups based on your interests (e.g. education, writing, yoga, etc.), and go to as many conferences as possible.

I used to go to conferences to learn. Now I go to conferences to connect. Not only do I learn a lot more, but my network exponentially grows as does my value.

The days of the isolated educator are coming to a close. This modern-day world is connected and global. If you are not joining in, you are not only missing out, you are also less effective.

We ask ourselves to read wide and read deep, but do we?

> Not all readers are leaders,
> but all leaders are readers.
>
> —HARRY S TRUMAN

I love to learn and read. So I model it via the blog and podcast. When I was a principal, when I was an AP, instructional coach, or a teacher, I constantly talked about what I was reading and how it was impacting me.

There is a ton of ways to learn. Maybe you enjoy video content more or you are a hands-on type of guy or gal.

That is all fine and dandy. The important part as a leader is to never stop learning and to share what you are learning with others.

It is inspiring.

Sure, know your audience. Maybe not everybody is into custom-made wooden business cards Jeff Dawidowski creates at old27.com.

But someone will find this fascinating. Find more of those type of people, dig in, and go deep. Seeing someone in a flow state is amazing to behold and share. Get there as often as you can, and give away what you learn.

As a school leader, be public about your learning. Get your hands dirty alongside your people analyzing data and designing interventions. Share what you learn, and tap into your teacher's heart. Like Gandhi and sugar.

I created a Facebook Live video retelling a popular story about Gandhi. There is a link in the resources page for this book, but I will quickly tell it here, too.

A mother was beside herself and did not quite know how to get her son to stop eating sugar. Because Gandhi was widely respected within her community and by her son, she resolved to bring her son to Gandhi and ask him to tell the son to quit sugar.

The mother and her son walk hours to find Gandhi. When they do, she expresses her concern to him and makes her request.

Gandhi smiles and tells the mother and her son to come back in a week.

Frustrated by the long trip they just took to meet Gandhi only to be given no help, the mom agrees to come back in a week and make the trek again because she knows that of all the people in the world, her son will listen to Gandhi.

After a week, the mother and her son make the hours-long walk to Gandhi again. When they meet him, he gently tells the son to quit sugar.

Confused, the mom wonders, "Why did we wait a week and make this long walk again just to have you tell my son what you could have told him last week?"

To this Gandhi replies, "I had to quit eating sugar first." Do not ask anyone to do anything you are not willing to do yourself.

Stop Reading Books about Education

You need a new set of eyeglasses. The old glasses you bought at the optometrist are worn out. You have not noticed in years because you continue to see the world in the same way, but what you really need is a fresh perspective.

Hello, Warby Parker! Warby Parker completely disrupted the eyeglasses industry. They saw a problem (pun intended): purchasing a pair of glasses was an incredibly costly process . . . but did it have to be?

As a college student, one of the Warby Parker founders lost a pair of glasses while traveling by plane. He thought to himself, *This sucks*, and *Why do glasses have to be soooo expensive?*

The thing is . . . nice-looking glasses do not have to be expensive. Instead of dropping north of $250 on a pair of glasses at your optometrist, you could purchase a pair from Warby Parker for $95.

If we continue to read books just about education, we do not see what we do not see. It is hard to get outside of our own head and get a fresh perspective if we use the same lens we have been looking through for an eternity. That is why in my mastermind, we read books outside of the education industry. Books that will push and develop us while changing our perspective.

In fact, many of the books we read in the mastermind are mentioned on the podcast. You can get a list of all the books mentioned on the podcast from the resource page for this book. You can also check out Episode 100, where I share my "Top 12 Leadership Books" and on my website, I have a popular post: "22 Books Every School Leader Should Read." All of these posts are linked for you on this book's resource page.

Serve Lunch and Sweep Floors

I really appreciate Matt Arend. I think Gandhi would be proud of him. His motto is "Never ask people to do something you aren't willing to do yourself." Well done, Matt. That idea is noted and in the books.

One way I connected with kids and staff in a nontraditional way as principal was by serving lunch and sweeping floors. Do not get me wrong. I did not do this every day by a long shot. I also did not see it as the best use of my time and how I could bring value to the organization. Occasionally, it was a great use of my time, though, and I enjoyed the relationships built from this investment.

SERVE LUNCH

I asked our cafe manager, Lori, what was the busiest day for her team. "That's easy," she said. "Kids go crazy on nacho day."

"Put me down for the next nacho day." Lori and her team could not believe it when I showed up to serve on nacho day. In fact, Lori tried to put me on fruits and veggies on the line instead of nachos! Knowing what she was doing, I let her know that I could handle "the heat in the kitchen." Twenty or so minutes later, roughly five-hundred 7th graders were successfully served. I had a better understanding of the demands of a cafe worker's job, and I had the opportunity to connect with kids in a different way around the school.

SWEEP FLOORS

My most important role as a principal was as an instructional leader. Therefore, I valued being in classes and providing feedback to teachers over all other tasks. It was absolutely maddening that in the last district I served, my leadership team (all three counselors and three APs) had lunch duty every single day.

Talk about a waste of money, time, and talent! I would have preferred to have staffed two APs and cut one. With the third's salary, I could have hired a whole team to manage the cafeteria for safety and cleanliness. Meanwhile the APs could have been in classrooms also conducting observations, providing feedback, and moving the vision of the school forward. But what do I know? The reality was, this institutional expectation was not changing anytime soon, and my APs and counselors were stuck in the lunch period every single day. At the end of lunch, they swept the cafe clean. Again, not a great use of their time, talents, or salary, but since they did it, I would chip in from time to time as well. Again, not every day, but I wanted people to know I was not "above" that task. The amazing additional benefit was that I also got to connect with our head engineer while cleaning the cafe. He taught me a lot of the history of the building, valuable information I would not have come across another way.

CHAPTER 7 NEXT STEPS

- ☐ Start an ed camp.

- ☐ Reflect: Are you willing to do (or currently doing) what you expect of your staff?

- ☐ Identify your school's nacho day, and serve!

CHAPTER EIGHT

Digital Impact

Digitouch and Impactical

Digitouch: Digital + Touch (v) To touch lives through digital means. When an individual lives in an authentic way and inspires a tribe of people to make the world a better place. Ryan Jackson has an impressive digitouch via his blog, *The Underdogs Advocate*.

Impactical: Impact + Digital (adj). Jethro Jones hosts an impactical podcast, *The Transformative Principal*.

How would you measure your digitouch? It has never been easier to make a contribution and inspire a tribe of people. You can go the amateur route and grab a free website and have dannysunshine.wordpress.com or you can invest a few dollars and turn pro with dannysunshine.com. Neither way is right or wrong, but the ability to "launch" and consistently create content that inspires has never been easier.

Getting noticed is the challenge. To do that, you must love your work. You must care for what you believe in and let your principles guide you (even if it takes an unpopular stance).

Viewing your work as art helps. Imagine creating a blog post that inspires someone to do bigger and better things than you ever thought possible. That is a pretty neat idea. And that is what art does. It inspires others to go out there and be great.

So how would you measure your digitouch? Are you an impactical leader?

The only reason you are reading this book right now is because of my digitouch. I have a podcast and a website where I share my viewpoint on education, leadership, and life, literally with the world.

Some of those messages hit and inspire a bunch of others. Some not so much. The key is to do it. To show up and put yourself out there. Nothing magical happens when you keep all those great ideas to yourself.

So what mode will you choose? Website? Podcast? What is your social media of choice? Twitter and Voxer are incredibly popular for educators, but they hang out on Facebook, Instagram, Snapchat, LinkedIn, and Pinterest, too. Jump online. Make an impact. Share your brilliant ideas (and not so brilliant ones).

Be impactical!

Slack Instead of Email

We need to communicate more effectively. And email sucks. It sucks as a communication tool, and it sucks our time away from what is most important . . . meaningful and deep work.

Here are a few things I hate about email:

> **BCC**—a tool for the weak and spineless. It is like talking about someone when they are not there. Are you sending an email and BCCing your boss? Do it in the light. Be transparent. Do not hide and be weak. That is so fake.

"Reply ALL"—Never reply all when offering a personal opinion or sharing personal information. This happens all the time. It is embarrassing, unprofessional, and often passive aggressive. Are you upset about something? Have a conversation.

It is too easy. It is much easier for me to tell you to do something (or tell you off) hiding behind a computer screen than having a conversation. Be brave. Be humane. Have the conversation.

It is too connected. You have permission to have a life.

It is inefficient for discussion. Important conversations are buried within every other message in a place synonymous with hell, *your inbox.* That important discussion with department chairs? Yes, search for it through the rest of the communication . . . emails from parents, the school board, your staff, students, family, consultants . . . the list goes on and on . . .

It has replaced thoughtful communication. Have you ever thought, *You should know this . . . I sent it in an email*? Just because you send information through an email does not mean that the message has landed. It probably has not stuck like you wished it had. Have face-to-face conversations. Make videos. Post a message in multiple places with multiple formats. Now you have a better chance of landing your message.

It prioritizes other people's priorities. The inbox is a place where I tell you what is important. If you start your day scrolling through your inbox and reading what is "urgent," you are now doing that work. What happened to that big goal you wanted to achieve today? Forget about it. There is a better way.

One important feature of Slack is in the idea of "channels." Channels can be thought of as different "rooms" where specific discussions happen. In the example below, I am using Slack with the audio editor of my podcast. You will notice on the right, we are having a discussion about podcasts and the release schedule.

I highlighted the "channels" in pink. For my media company, each podcast I produce has its own "channel." That way my editor and I know where and what show we are discussing at any given point. It keeps us focused on the content that needs to be discussed. I will explain how I used it in the school setting.

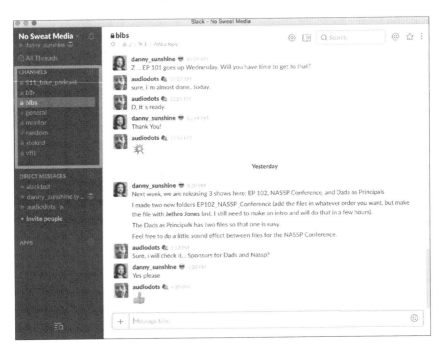

How I Used Slack within a School

For my school, I set up channels as different Response to Intervention (RtI) rooms. When students struggled, they may have been at Level 2 or Level 3 status and in need of more intense interventions. Each struggling student had their own room (channel) where I could discuss their current level of success with the RtI team and the specific student's teachers. This allowed us to be on the same page. Not only did we discuss, but we also shared files and the work that needed to be completed within the "channel" or "room" for a specific student. The beauty of Slack is that once you add people to an individual channel, you do not have to add them again. This makes communication much more efficient.

How would I use Slack in a school?

In addition to RtI, I would add channels for anything important within a school:

1. PBIS
2. Celebrating Staff
3. Discipline
4. General "Nuts and Bolts"
5. Events (sports, clubs, etc.)
6. PLC teams
7. Community

The sky is really the limit here.

And the beauty of channels is that you can add whomever you want. It can be staff-wide, or you can set up a room just for your leadership team to discuss.

Why does that matter? It is a one-stop-shop where all your internal discussions can be had quickly. Then you know that email will only be for parents, community, and central office (and spam).

All internal communication could be done within Slack.

By setting up specific channels, you allow people to read what is relevant to them. For example, Mrs. K. does not care much for sports, but she does care about the school's PLC initiative. Now she does not have to scan through the newsletter for information she cares about. She can go directly to the PLC channel and can avoid the Sports channel altogether.

Put yourself out there. Gone are the days where you need to know someone to get noticed and or climb some type of communication ladder to get the word out.

Putting yourself out there is simple in theory. Blogs, vlogs, and podcasts all have a low bar for entry and all even have a free entrance ticket if you want to go cheap.

So, what makes it difficult? Saying something that matters. Getting clear on your voice. Offering something valuable to your tribe. Staying consistent. Ignoring the haters (in the comments) and the negative voice that exists in all our minds. Sometimes just starting is the most challenging part.

Other folks mention, "There are hundreds or thousands of [THE TOPIC THAT INTERESTS YOU] blogs already . . . it is a crowded space. Why would anyone care to hear from me?" That is easy. **Because there is only one you.** You are the only one who has had your unique set of experiences that has shaped your opinion and formed the lens through which you view the world. And that perspective matters a lot. Come to think of it, not sharing your voice is an awfully selfish thing to do. We all benefit when you put yourself out there via a blog, vlog, or podcast.

I do not have 10,000 or 100,000 raving fans. I am not even sure that I have 1,000 raving fans. I do know that I serve 39 clients (at the time of this writing) in my masterminds. I think they are raving fans. I married my best friend in July of 2017. She is a raving fan. That is all that matters to me. Can I serve and love these people well? If I do, then I have made a difference.

The point I am trying to make is that would it be worth it for you to start a blog, vlog, or podcast if you dramatically impacted the life of one, five, 10, 100 or more individuals? It is worth it to me. When I started my podcast, I hoped that the show would grow, but in all honesty, even if no one listened, I would continue.

Why? That is because I have learned so much from talking to great leaders. I have changed. I have grown. It has been worth it for my own personal development. I probably will never see as many downloads as Tim Ferriss or sell as many books as Seth Godin. That is okay. My goal is to be the best version of myself, help a bunch of people, and be creative doing things I enjoy. Podcasting has also given me the gift of better self-awareness and a clear idea of who I am, who I help, and where I am going. This clarity in my personal and professional life is priceless; I only got there by consistently putting myself out there. My best advice: Just do you. *And start.*

The Power of You

You are now a brand, or at least you should think of yourself that way. The world is much more connected these days and parents, staff, and students are watching you . . . the school leader. So when they look, what do they see? Or are you incredibly private with absolutely no digital footprint?

Ryan Jackson is getting this thing right. You can check him out on underdogsadvocate.com, Twitter (@RyanBJackson1), and Instagram (@rbjackson4791566).

Why is Ryan getting it right? Because he is absolutely a brand and you know exactly what he stands for. This is a *huge* benefit to his school because it attracts other innovators, businesses, potential employees, and other people who want to help him and the school he leads (currently at Mt. Pleasant) be a success. What does he stand for? Take five minutes and you know what Ryan is about:

1. STEAM
2. Innovation
3. #UnderdogsAdvocate
4. #FitLeaders
5. and much more . . .

He is an incredible inspiration to me and many other educators through his branding and the content he produces on social media and his blog.

He has also been on the podcast two times on Episodes 6 and 50.

Not only does his school benefit from this leader who "gets it," I am absolutely positive that he is opening doors he never thought he would walk through providing him amazing and lucrative future opportunities.

So, who are you? What is your brand? Are you sharing your personality through your newsletter, your blog, and social media? What do you stand for?

If I took five minutes to search you out, would I have a clear answer? Should I? Does this even matter?

CHAPTER 8 NEXT STEPS

☐ A theme is emerging . . . put yourself out there.
Start a blog, vlog, or podcast, and post frequently to
gain clarity on your vision and refine your voice.

☐ Experiment with Slack or another app like Voxer
to improve communication within your school.

☐ Ditch email. It is a time suck and does
not produce meaningful work.

CHAPTER NINE

Loving Others

Love Freely

I believe we would all benefit from adding more humanity to our work including love. I believe that people would give more of themselves if they simply knew that you cared. Chad Weiden (Episode 32) accomplishes this is by strolling through the halls and prioritizing conversations and connection. He puts his phone away and asks his staff how they are doing . . . and actually listens. He is present and does not think about what he needs to say in response. He just sits. And listens.

Teachers feel heard through this simple demonstration of active listening, and they know he cares.

Jeff Zoul (Episodes 27 & 107) does this by writing old-fashioned, handwritten thank-you cards to his staff. He did this as a principal, as an assistant superintendent of teaching and learning, and now as a leader in the ConectEDD / What Great Educators Do Differently Movement (WGEDD).

Jimmy Casas (Episode 107) did this as a principal by sending thank-you cards home to the spouses or parents of his staff members. In the note, he mentioned what a gift they were to his community and shared a specific example of how they made the community better (he is also Jeff's partner leading the ConectEDD / WGEDD movement).

Hamish Brewer (bonus episode on the podcast) demonstrates love through turning the picture of a principal on its head. He may be one of the most relatable principals out there, and his students adore him. You can often catch Hamish skateboarding through the halls of his school and telling kids how important they are to him.

Fran McGreevy (Episode 69) did this by constantly sharing at staff meetings that he felt he was among "gods and goddesses." Fran is an encourager . . . a necessary skill in education where staff often gets beat down until the respite of the summer helps them recharge and rejuvenate. But under Fran's care, staff felt alive and thrived. He was able to see the gold in each person, and he boldly called it out each day to inspire his staff to their best.

Marlena Gross-Taylor (Episode 21) did this by spending time helping first-year teachers set up classrooms or organize classrooms after a tough day.

Connie Hamilton (Episode 62 & 110) is experimenting with this in her district by understanding her staff's "Love Languages" and making sure she communicates with them in a way that shows she cares.

Would you ever consider telling your staff, "I love you"?

Maybe you do not have to be that candid, but I truly believe your people would go further for your community if they knew how much you cared.

"People won't care how much you know, until they know how much you care."

GIVE GIFTS. BE GENEROUS.

Each year when my staff filled out their emergency forms, I would ask what their favorite snack was. This was a clandestine attempt to have in my back pocket at least one go-to gift I could give my staff.

Times I enjoyed giving gifts included:

1. Holidays
2. Birthdays
3. Anniversaries
4. Any other time to celebrate ...
5. If I knew a staff member was dealing with something tough outside of work

I want you to close your eyes and think of the stereotypical manly gym teacher ...

I will never forget when I went into Matt's gym class with a bag full of gummy worms. Matt is probably 6'2", a towering man that is bald with a fashionable beard.

Tears formed in his eyes and he gave me the biggest bear hug ever after he looked into the bag and saw the gift.

"Dan ... those are my favorite ... Thank You!"

I nearly broke in half while receiving the bear hug.

"You're welcome" ... I whispered after having the air crushed out of me.

I remember when Christina's dad was battling cancer. No words could make her father better, but I wanted her to know that I cared. Cheezits were her favorite snack, and combined with a note, "Feel free to come chat with me if you need to get anything off your chest" was the most compassionate gesture I could make to her.

Giving gifts does not have to be elaborate, but given just a little work and research, a school leader can give a perfect gift and demonstrate a little generosity and compassion throughout the day.

Now, in the Mastermind, I act generously in a different way. A few current members referred some amazing educators that committed to joining the mastermind. As a result, I sent them gifts that showed how much I cared for them. Brandon loves technology, so he received an Amazon Echo. Nick is a huge golf fan, so I sent him 50 of his favorite golf balls personalized with his name and school. I learned this from my mentor Aaron Walker. Do not send a gift with your logo and name all over it. Make it all about the receiver. Not only will they love a personalized gift, they will think of you every time they use it. Finally, Eileen is a huge crossword lover, and to my surprise, she had never subscribed to a year of the *NY Times Crossword* app. So that was her personal gift. Cost does not matter. Making it personal does.

PERSONALIZE WHAT YOU GIVE YOUR STAFF.

Think about this in two ways. **One,** personalize your PD for teachers. Avoid at all costs "one-size-fits all" professional development. As a school leader, we push our staff to avoid this type of teaching, but we often fall back on this type of PD. I am guessing that is because of a lack of planning and imagination.

How can you do better? Form a team and delegate the task of offering personalized PD to your staff.

The PD@Brooks team did just that for us, and the result was much better received and relevant PD. Teachers that feel like they are being developed and have tools to better serve their students are the type of teachers we dream of working with, yet we often disengage and drown teachers in the boring bureaucratic hell that is school. Stop it. You can do better.

Two. Personalize gifts, memos, and thank-you cards. Get to know your staff through 15-minute short interviews, and repeat as often as possible with quick check-ins. Review your notes often and invest your money or time in personal notes or gifts. The time you take to go the extra mile will pay off.

For example, I love tea, but very specific types. Not all tea is created equal. And one Christmas, when I received a box of Lipton tea, I threw it in the bottom right drawer of my desk, where it stayed for two years until I tossed it in the garbage when I moved to a new school. Of course, I appreciated the person's gesture, but the Lipton tea was like making a layup with no defense around on the basketball court. Now imagine that the gift giver gave me a can of Green Matcha from the Republic of Tea. That would have been like when Michael Jordan dunked over Patrick Ewing.

BUY YOUR ENEMIES GIFTS.

I do not practice this, but this advice has been given to me twice. I balked both times. And writing about it is helping me process the idea.

My friend Bret Barnhart first mentioned this idea on a sunny drive in Tennessee on my way to the Nashville airport. We had just finished a face-to-face mastermind meet-up. The weekend had rocked my world, business deals were made, and relationships were nourished.

I explained to him how I felt mistreated and that my character was attacked at work. This bullying and intimidation led to a handful of leaders resigning and one even took a long-term medical leave.

Bret's advice, "You should buy your supervisor a gift."

Forget that.

My body and soul revolted at the idea of doing something kind in this situation. What I wanted was blood and revenge—an equally poor idea at the other end of the spectrum.

Wondering how I should handle my final end-of-year review, I asked my mastermind if I should even show up.

Overall, the advice was the same. Show up. Leave on a good note. Do what is expected of you.

Tom offered helpful advice: "The only way she can hurt you with the evaluation is if she rolled it up and hit you with it."

I agree to an extent and appreciate Tom's heart. However, one has to develop a good amount of mental toughness to face lies and character attacks and walk away unscathed . . . and I was just a principal in an elite area of Houston. I cannot imagine what it is like to be a celebrity or the POTUS!

And then Aaron shared, "You know what I would do, Danny . . . you are not going to like it . . . I would buy her an intentional gift."

What the heck?

Why are we talking about gifts again for someone who caused so much pain and anguish in my life?

Forget that.

I considered buying a meaningful leadership book and sharing it at my end-of-year review, but I just could not bring myself to do it.

I think Bret and Aaron were trying to share with me three ideas:

- how to make peace with a troubling reality
- acting in a way that is above reproach
- changing your heart through generosity

This last point is the most important. The idea of acting generously toward a professional bully was more for me than for them. Bret and Aaron wanted my heart to change.

Well, guys, I think through writing and meditation (and business success), I found my healing. I am a thrifty guy so sorry, no book, no gift.

Like I said, I never did it, but I wanted to share with you in case you might benefit. Maybe you are a bigger person than I am!

Positive Messages

I read *Search Inside Yourself* with my mastermind clients in the Spring of 2017. We loved that book for many reasons, but one idea that really stuck out is the importance of the messages we tell ourselves as well as the messages we tell others.

In the book, the author discusses how individuals need to use a 3:1 ratio of positive to negative messages. The stakes are even higher at home. In marriage, the relationship is 5:1.

This means our positive messaging is incredibly important.

Negative messages stick with us.

They leave residue that is hard to shake off. I remember watching *Ghostbusters* in a movie theater in the '80s with other kids. We laughed hysterically when a ghost "slimed" one of the protagonists leaving an icky, green residue all over them. That is exactly what negative messages do (especially when sent without compassion). They "slime" the other individual with a nasty residue that can take days, weeks, even years to clean off.

In my humble opinion, life is hard enough. As a leader, I want to be chief encourager. I want people to know that they are appreciated, admired, and even loved. I think the best organizations operate as a family. There is trust, compassion, and a shared sense of belonging and identity.

One way to build that bond is through positive messaging.

You can do that obviously through your words, but I like to write handwritten cards personalized to the recipient.

Here is exactly what I admire about you . . .

Want another idea?

Joshua Spodek, my guest on Episode 079, once wrote 70 gratitude emails to friends.

What he learned:

- This was a hard activity and required much thought.
- He realized how much he had been helped.
- Relationships he cared about he let languish.
- Gratitude is an exercise of vulnerability for the writer.
- This exercise helped Joshua go deeper . . . what was the meaning and results beyond what the person did for him.

What is a Person?

There is a sickness inside all of us as leaders. If we do not temper it, the sickness creates a box that the staff gets stuck inside. The sickness is judgment informed by pessimism.

We all know the idea of the glass half full or half empty. If I am honest, too often I find myself in a negative mindset focused on the problems that lie ahead. In any given negative situation, I feel sorry for myself and wonder why the universe is conspiring to ruin and maybe even kill me.

On my best days, I am filled optimism, positivity, and joy.

When I bathe myself in gratitude and share this with people I lead, it is truly a gift. The biggest compliment ever paid to me at my former school was from a counselor, Michelle. She mentioned one day as I sat in her office, "Danny, you brought a sense of calm that was so needed in this building."

To date, that has been one of the nicest things ever said about me.

Mindset matters. What kind of introspective, tough, deep work are you engaged in so that you share compassion, gratitude, and generosity with your staff? As leaders, our organizations take on aspects of our personality. Are you proud of how the organization is reflecting you?

The next time you look at one of your staff members, I challenge you to look for their best qualities.

I dare you to enter into a dialogue with someone who often opposes your viewpoint. Naturally, it may be difficult to see the positive traits this person brings to the table. Probably the human default is to see this opponent as an adversary, worse yet, an enemy. But you have to fight. In fact, if you don't fight the illness you are rooted in close-mindedness.

Viewed as an adversary, how can her talents be leveraged to benefit the community? Vilified, what is this person's value?

How should we view our staff? What is more promising?

What they are or what they are not?

CHAPTER 9 NEXT STEPS

☐ Get to really know your staff and do your best to find them personalized gifts.

☐ Although gifts are a great way to express appreciation, that is not the only way. Take time to write a personalized "Thank-You" note or gratitude email like Josh Spodek.

☐ Leaders are natural problem solvers, but they suffer from the "Tetris effect." If your default is identifying and solving problems, you'll see mostly problems. Do your best to identify the positive in your people and not just what needs to be improved.

CHAPTER TEN

Empathy

Teaching Empathy

Empathy may be the most critical characteristic of success. And our students may be losing this skill . . .

I see many folks concerned that empathy is decreasing among students because of their incessant use of smartphones. Empathy is decreasing and narcissism is increasing because children are glued to their screens instead of engaging in face-to-face conversations.

Personally, I am not so sure this is true.

I just think it is a new technology that is changing how we behave, and that scares adults. I think we'll just adjust as a society. Television did not kill radio or movies. We adjusted. E-readers did not kill tangible books. We adjusted.

I observe students still connecting through their smartphones and sharing these experiences with their peers sitting beside them.

But the point of this topic is to explore empathy. If empathy is a critical skill students need to master, how do we teach it?

When I was an AVID teacher, my students participated in an experience called *Walk a Mile in My Shoes*. This kind of activity increases empathic awareness because empathy improves when one can see from another's perspective. Some questions you might want students to explore are:

- What brings water to my eyes?
- What situations cause knots in my stomach?
- Who am I as a person? What do I stand for?

You can see where these questions are going, and I am sure you can develop more questions for your students to explore. After completing the activity, students would share their responses. This kind of dialogue helps all students understand (just a little bit more) where their peers are coming from. I came across an activity shared by the Jesuit Schools Network where participants engage in a simulation of a refugee's experience. Talk about powerful! I can only imagine how much one would learn about a refugee's experience by engaging in this activity. When I was a senior at the University of Illinois at Urbana-Champaign, Professor Willis led our class through a "Walk a Mile in My Shoes" activity. It was amazing how much I learned about my classmates. Professor Willis instructed us to take a step forward if the statement she read was true:

- Step forward if you have never been pulled over by the police.
- Step forward if no one in your family has been incarcerated.
- Step forward if your parents went to college.

I remember connecting with peers when Prof. Willis asked us, "Step forward if someone in your family has NOT been incarcerated." I stepped forward, but a number of my peers remained where we had once stood shoulder to shoulder. By physically stepping forward and leaving my peers behind me, I literally saw my privilege in relation to others for the first time. The feeling was visceral. My heart hurt for my peers.

What an incredible dialogue starter!

I encourage you to search online for more activities. If you want to increase empathy in your classroom, help your students walk a mile in someone else's shoes. All these activities can be equally powerful done with students or staffs.

While writing the first draft of this book, I read Joshua Spodek's *Leadership Step By Step.*

This is required leadership reading.

The first ¾ of the book is focused on the reader's inner world—their beliefs at the foundation of their soul that really motivate our actions.

I think Spodek's idea is that first an individual truly needs to understand what motivates her before she can learn to motivate and lead others. The last ¼ of the book is how to lead others.

Here is where Spodek teaches us to increase our empathy:

- Chapter 16 taught me the exercise "Meaningful Connection," which I explain below.
- Chapter 17 introduced the "Make People Feel Understood" exercise.
- Chapter 18 is a gem that says, "Lead with Empathy."

All these exercises will improve your ability to listen, understand, and empathize with all people. With this strong foundation you then have permission to lead.

Think about it.

Who are the leaders you most admired?

Now think about those leaders that you *despised.*

What sets them apart? I believe a distinguishing feature between and excellent and poor leader is their ability to understand what drives you . . . what your passions are . . .

And those leaders who had no idea who you were at the core . . .

Those leaders who even invalidated your passions . . .

You did not stick around there long. Did you?

I will briefly describe the steps of "Meaningful Connection" script and provide an example, but you will need to read Spodek's book to go get "Make People Feel Understood," "Lead with Empathy," and the other incredible content. If you are reading this because you work harder than most at improving your leadership craft, then you will absolutely love this book.

If I suggested just one book for you to read this year, this would be it.

Meaningful Connection

- Ask an individual's passion.
- Your partner will respond with a surface-level answer.
- Go deeper and say, "Great . . . I know [some you know] who [does X] for [their reason] and I know [another person] who [does Y] for [their reason]. Why do you do [your partner's passion]?"
- Listen for the handful of words that are unique and stressed.
- Respond to what they said in order to clarify and make sure you **use their exact word choice**.

Example

If I was talking to my mentor, Aaron Walker, this conversation might go like this . . .

Me: "So, Aaron . . . what do you consider your passion?"

Think of a heavy southern drawl for Aaron's part . . .

Aaron: "Well, Sunshine, I want to teach men to lead lives of success and significance."

Me: "That's great, Aaron. I know that Gary Vee leads and wants to create a Honey Empire because he wants to treat people incredibly well while absolutely dominating his industry. I know that Larry Page leads to solve billion-person problems for lasting impact and to improve humans' experiences worldwide. Why do you lead so that men learn to lead lives of success and significance?"

Aaron: "Great question, Sunshine. Success is actually relatively easy to attain. I also find that success does not bring lasting *meaning to my life*. When I ran over a pedestrian in 2001, I went into a deep depression. It took me a while, but when I emerged from my depression, my focus was a lot sharper. When I leave this world, I am not taking anything with me. Not my house or any of my riches. So I am focused on *leaving a legacy*."

Me: "So what I am hearing is that you are focused on living a meaningful life and leaving a legacy that will continue to inspire society after you are gone . . ."

My Thoughts on this Exercise

This script works because it moves from surface level to deep and authentic conversation. By sharing examples of people you know and the reason they do their passions, you communicate that you care and are interested in a real answer. Through active listening and using the actual words that your partner shares, you communicate that you were truly listening and care about what their passions are. This compassion allows you to demonstrate and grow your empathy.

One More Note on Empathy

What does your community really need? One definition of empathy that I really like is understanding what someone else needs. What are their wants, desires, challenges, fears, and dreams? If you understand that, you have empathy.

Perspective is everything. The idea of walking a mile in someone else's shoes is the exact activity and skill set that every leader needs to be fully empathetic.

How do I know?

Because I am sometimes terrible at it.

It's easy (and cowardly) to think and say, "Do it because I am the boss" or "You should know that; I put it in the email."

These perspectives are egocentric, focused on what you have done in any given situation while ignoring the other person completely.

I can be empathetic, but if I am honest, that sometimes is based on whether I like you or not. It is much more difficult to be empathetic with people I do not like. Again, a selfish approach. It is all about me.

I need to change that.

I limit my own leadership capacity when I do not consider the rich diversity of experience that my people bring to the table.

The metaphor of an iceberg and the water captures empathy perfectly.

What we see on the outside are results of what is going on the inside and sometimes mask exactly what is going on. We do not know unless we ask what is going on. If we do not get an answer, then we can ask ourselves what we **think** is going on and at the very least think from another person's perspective.

Figure this crucial piece of leadership out and you have a solid chance of being a success and the exact leader your community needs.

CHAPTER 10 NEXT STEPS

☐ Do an empathy-building exercise like "Walk a Mile in My Shoes" or "Meaningful Connection."

☐ Before opening your mouth, listen! Reflect what you hear and ask, "Correct me if I am wrong, but what I hear is . . ." If you are corrected, say, "Thank you" and try to rephrase. Don't stop until the other person says, "That's right." In every situation, consider these things:

- What is the other person thinking right now?

- What is the other person feeling right now?

- What is the other person wanting right now?

CHAPTER ELEVEN

Time Management

What Do You Focus On? What Do You Ignore?

Cal Newport wrote an incredibly helpful and challenging book called, *Deep Work*. We read this text in the mastermind in May–June of 2017. The whole premise is easy to understand, but much harder to implement. Extended Amounts of Time + Extreme Focus = Remarkable Results. The book offers a number of strategies and mental models that you can apply to get remarkable results. They all boil down to the question, "What do you choose to focus on, and what do you choose to ignore?" We live in a busy world where everything is screaming, "Look at me . . . I need your attention."

Take your smartphone (assuming you have one), for example.

These tech tools are expertly designed to keep you glued to the phone . . . so much so, you might even go into withdrawal if you stopped checking social media and email.

I have gone through a few iterations of how to declutter and de-notify my phone so that I could accomplish more deep work.

A few rules to consider (for the iPhone):

- When possible, keep your phone off.
- When it's turned on, use the **Do Not Disturb** mode. Keep your partner, children, and any other VIPs as **Favorites**. This way, their calls can still get through to you in emergencies.
- Turn off all notifications including all dings, red bubbles with numbers, and pop-ups.
- Remove email from your phone.
- Remove all social media from your phone (except your favorite one. Use the computer for the rest of social media).
- Look at your app use. Any app you have not used this week, delete.
- Drop all your apps into one folder and keep it on your second screen. Keep a motivating image or quote that will inspire you to focus or make a significant contribution to your community and the world today. I created a free motivating wallpaper for your phone available in the book's resource page.

In all honesty, I do everything above except four and five. Since I now run an online business, I tell myself I need to stay connected to offer value and build my brand. I am not sure if this is true or a lie, but it is a tension I feel.

My home screen currently is a picture of when I got engaged to Miriam in New Orleans.

It reminds me, especially at home, to connect with Miriam in real life rather than looking at her on my phone! What a crazy reminder to need, but it works!

If you would like help focusing, making better decisions, and accomplishing more in 12 weeks than most people do in 12 months, let me know. I want to help.

Email me at daniel@betterleadersbetterschools.com and I can send you information of when I am hosting my next productivity webinar. I will help you break down productivity myths and build up positive mental frameworks that will help you increase your impact.

BUILD YOUR BOLLINGEN TOWER

Serving lunch and sweeping floors, although noble tasks to complete occasionally, are the antithesis of what Cal Newport would call "deep work."

And as a school leader, you are called to engage in deep work. I am arguing that nothing is more important. As I have mentioned before, not every task is important, and emergencies are rarely actual emergencies.

Email can hijack your schedule faster than you can finish this sentence and rob you from accomplishing anything meaningful.

The antidote then is to build your own version of Bollingen Tower, the structure that Carl Jung built so that he could engage in deep work. What made this place important is that it was incredibly isolated and protected Jung from all distractions.

1. As a school leader, we cannot shut ourselves out from the community, but we can do a few things to increase our chances of engaging in deep work: Have a closed-door policy from time to time. Ask your APs to handle any emergencies that pop up. Do the same for them increasing their ability to complete deep work.

2. Turn off all notifications from your phone.

3. Run your phone in Do Not Disturb Mode. Your favorites can still get through in emergencies.

4. Remove all apps from the home screen of your phone. Put all apps on one folder labeled "Focus."

5. Turn off notifications on your computer.

6. Be visible during most of the day outside of deep work hours so people see you as still accessible.

7. Create an atmosphere in your office free of clutter and distraction. It should be welcoming and warm, and it should promote long stretches of focus.

8. Do not multitask.

If you create a version of Jung's Bollingen Tower in your school office, I believe you will be a few steps closer to accomplishing more than you ever have in your career.

UNPLUG

It is really hard to find time for yourself, for reflection, and for deep work. Basically everyone comes to you to solve *their* problem as a school leader.

That is, if you let them.

We must empower people to solve their own problems.

My wife taught me, "You teach people how you want to be treated." That quote actually hurt at the time of hearing it although that was not her objective. I was going through a particularly tough challenge at work, and she was encouraging me to establish boundaries and clearly communicate to my supervisor what I needed. Sometimes we have to unplug from relationships in order to be fully effective.

Other times we need to unplug from our phones. Earlier in the book, I mentioned *Deep Work*, by Cal Newport. Another idea that he proposed in his book that I would like to share with you here is the idea of an internet and tech device Sabbath.

As I noted earlier, it is powerful (and peaceful) to clean your home screen from the clutter of the 1,000 apps you barely even use but still keep on your phone. It is even more powerful to turn off notifications and noises from your phone as well. For me, at the center of turning notifications off was a battle with my own ego. Parts of my brain light up and release chemicals into my body shouting, "You are important," every time I receive a new notification. Turning them off has been a great practice in quenching my ego as well. Not only will your ego subside, your concentration will flourish, and you will have the opportunity to really focus. Maybe you will be able to focus for the first time in a long time. Plus, if you want to become more creative and generate better ideas, then you should purposely pursue unplugging and welcome boredom. A 2014 study in the *Journal of Experimental Social Psychology* found that bored people are more prone to "divergent thinking styles," an advantage for any leader. When I was a kid, I dreamed up the wildest scenarios that I acted out each day. In a single day, I could be a superhero, pirate, or space explorer. By being unplugged naturally, I was able to generate wild fantasies and come up with creative ways to pass the time.

Embrace unplugging and welcome back that creative genius that lives inside you. You can thank me later when you get a raise or promotion because of that winning idea you created while bored.

IGNORE STUFF THAT DOES NOT MATTER

Guess what? Not everything matters, yet we sometimes act like it does. If you struggle focusing on "keeping the main thing the main thing," I have a productivity secret for you.

Introducing the Ideal Week

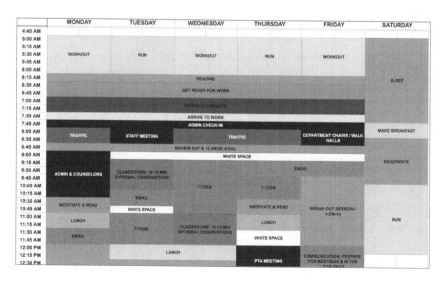

The Ideal Week is something I regularly use and teach in my productivity course. Essentially, an ideal week is just that, where an individual blocks off stretches of time to work on what is truly important (because not everything is). I go deeper in my productivity course, but here are the basics (which I learned from Brian Moran).

STRATEGIC BLOCK

Once a week for 1.5–3 hours. This is about vision. Where is the organization going? What are the dreams deferred? Too often as leaders, we have a wish list of agenda items that we never have been able to address. The main reason for that is focusing on everything else but the future. During a strategic block, focus on the future. Start making plans now.

NUTS AND BOLTS

Each day has items you need to accomplish. As a school leader, you need to constantly be in classrooms so you understand the pulse of the building and can offer constructive and encouraging feedback. Get those observations and other regular items on the calendar now.

BUFFER BLOCK

This time is slotted for the unimportant yet essential aspects of the job. The easiest way to increase your productivity and impact is to limit the amount of time spent on these tasks. Check email once or twice a day for 30–60 minutes. No more. Seriously. If you regularly check email, not only are you not engaged in "deep work," you also let everyone else set your agenda for the day. A study by Professor Gloria Mark at the University of California Irvine suggests that 28% of a professional's time is spent on interruptions and recovery. That is 11 hours of a 40-hour work week! Schedule in the time that you will sign vacation requests and process payroll. Be intentional about when this will occur, and you will not stress about getting it done because mentally you know where it fits in the schedule. So what is most important to focus on? That is really up to you. I teach my clients to focus on one to three big goals and show them a system on how to accomplish more in 12 weeks than most do in 12 months.

THE IDEAL WEEK

I do not actually remember where I learned The Ideal Week, but it has been an absolute game changer in my personal and professional life. It has become one of the most popular tactics I teach my clients. The Ideal Week is exactly that, a tool where you create how an ideal week would look before the week even begins.

Here are a few tips when getting started:

1. Time increments. I like blocking time in 15-minute chunks. Use what works for you; maybe it is as small as five minutes or bigger, like a 30-minute block.

2. Intentionally schedule when you will check email and do other low-level work. This will protect your time to work on important work during the rest of the day. I recommend one or two 30–60-minute blocks a day for email.

3. Schedule one 90–180-minute block for strategy. As the leader, you are responsible for the vision of the organization! Where are you going and how you are going to get there are important questions to explore. Figuring out a plan to accomplish your vision does not happen without intentional planning.

4. Prioritize and schedule all important tasks into your ideal week. There are only so many minutes each work week. How will you utilize this finite resource? Everything cannot be important!

5. If you find that you are not able to schedule everything in, you may have found a task that needs to be delegated. Who can you choose to carry the work forward?

6. Prioritize your personal life. I highly recommend scheduling time to connect with family and friends,

exercise, and participate in life-giving activities. Life and work goes in seasons. However, a leader who exists "in the red" only has herself to blame. Take care of yourself!

7. Remember that this tool is the ideal. Do not try to adhere to it perfectly, or you will be set up for big-time disappointment. Schedule white space into ideal week too so when blocks of activities need to be moved around, you have the flexibility.

Good luck!

The Miracle Morning

The Miracle Morning (TMM) was written by Hal Elrod and has been a monumental book in my life because it has given me a system he calls SAVERS where I can start each day with a win. Hal suggests completing each of the following components over the first hour of your morning. However, cater it to your needs. It can be short as six minutes (one minute per component) or as long as you would like and your schedule allows.

SILENCE

Start the day in silence and meditation. Personally, I read a chapter of Scripture each morning, and I enjoy using an app for meditation (I have found Headspace, Calm, Oak, and 10% Happier to be useful).

AFFIRMATION

Are you like me? Do you have a little negative voice in your head that likes to remind you of all your mistakes and what you can't do? Affirmations are an antidote to this negative voice. By starting your day affirming who you are, you positively frame the day.

I think of affirmations like a positive shock to my mental state. Feel free to download my resource page that accompanies this book to get the personal affirmations I recite each day.

VISUALIZATION

When I was a swimmer in high school, I had my first experience with visualization. Coach told us to climb to the top of the lockers, lie on our backs, and close our eyes. Next, he asked us to visualize the entire sectional state race including the preparation, the actual race, and postrace celebration. We thought of things like this:

- How do I need to prepare to be successful for this race?
- During the race I imagined every aspect . . .
  » The start
  » Each stroke in the water
  » Every breath I would take
  » Each turn under water
  » And a strong finish (milliseconds before the competition)

Visualization should be a key component of a successful day for school leaders, too.

Top performers visualize top performances each day.

Until now, each part of SAVERS has helped the individual implementing TMM mentally and emotionally. Exercise is the best way to give your body a jolt of physical energy.

My morning exercise consists of activities I enjoy:

- Walking, running, or riding my bike outside
- Walking on a steep incline on the treadmill
- High Intensity Interval Training (HIIT) for fat loss either running intervals, strength HIIT, or a combo
- Strength training

Recently, I have been engaged in CrossFit classes. I like the challenge, the variety, and the camaraderie found at my box (this is what CrossFit athletes call the gym where they work out). I find the benefits of exercise to be tremendous. Exercise helps me start the day feeling accomplished.

In fact, I get so much confidence from completing a rigorous morning workout that I feel I can accomplish anything! #beastmode

Other benefits include feeling more alert throughout the day as well as developing a nice physique (which also improves my confidence).

READING

Each morning, I read the Bible during the Silence phase of TMM. During the Reading phase of TMM, I read for personal development. At the time of writing this, I am reading *Deep Work* with my mastermind clients.

Do not skimp on this area of TMM. Readers are leaders. President Truman famously stated . . . **"Not all readers are leaders, but all leaders are readers."**

Not only do I read for personal development each morning, but on my best days, I also read for professional development. I try to schedule 15–20 minutes of this kind of reading during my ideal week.

SCRIBING

If reading encourages personal development, writing solidifies it. When I was an AVID teacher, I remember learning a fact that has always stuck with me: **Writing unlocks and activates more parts of the brain than any other activity.** In other words, writing makes you smarter because it is the most difficult cognitive task you can engage in any day. What to write? Here are a few ideas:

- Stream of consciousness
- Morning pages
- A blog post on any topic of interest
- Summary of what you read in the morning and how you will apply it to your life
- Five-minute journal (explained in the "Developing an Attitude of Gratitude podcast episode)

Each morning, I write in my gratitude journal. One question I answer is . . .

What would make today great?

This question helps me know what I want to accomplish. Visualization takes only a few minutes. During this time, I mentally complete the tasks of the day. This all happens in my mind.

If I have a meeting . . . how will I run it? How will the conversations go? How will I adapt to things thrown my way? And I do this for every *major* aspect of the day.

CHAPTER 11 NEXT STEPS

- [ ] Consider your relationship with your phone. What is one action you can take from this chapter (e.g. turning off notifications) that will help you unplug and focus?

- [ ] Tackle your office and build your personal Bollingen Tower.

- [ ] Create an ideal week, and connect with me if I can help you become more productive.

CHAPTER TWELVE

Goals

Get More Done and Stop Wasting Time

If we are absolutely honest when reflecting on how we spend time, probably most of us can agree that a lot of time is wasted, mismanaged, and generally misused. A major difference between me and most uber-successful people is that they use time a lot differently. They think about and leverage it at a much higher level. I came across an article on Medium called "Compounding Time." Here are six hacks that people like Warren Buffett, Einstein, and Oprah used to be successful:

1. Keep a journal.
2. Take regular naps.
3. Walk at least 15 minutes a day.
4. Read. Read. Read.
5. Have a "Conversation partner."
6. Perform experiments.

I am not there yet, but I have experimented on myself and developed a three-headed monster system that has exponentially increased my productivity and that of my students.

You can learn this system through a free webinar and go deeper with an actual online course if that is your fancy. Your productivity will soar if you execute my system. I guarantee it. You can join an ongoing webinar where I reveal, "My 'Secret System' How to Accomplish More in Life Without Working Around the Clock" by emailing me for the next session. Currently, I run them every two weeks, but if I stop for some reason, I can share a taped version of the webinar that will still benefit you.

The system I teach helped me write this book you are reading right now. It also helped me create the audio version in less than 12 weeks. During 12 weeks over the summer, I had three goals:

1. Add 10 mastermind clients.
2. Lose 2–4% body fat.
3. Write my first book for education.

Before I share my results, here is an excerpt from my journal recording if my system actually worked …

July 1, 2017

I am five weeks into my 12-week goals (I have seven more weeks). With nearly 50% of my time already incredibly focused, here are the results . . .

Add more mastermind clients

I have not added any yet, but the mastermind has been closed until now. I made personal videos for everyone on the mastermind waitlist. They have the opportunity to join the mastermind before I invite the 1,000 school leaders that receive my newsletter. I am feeling good about this goal. I can meet this goal through the waitlist alone and I know leaders that receive my email are hungry to join as well.

Lose 2–4% body fat

Five weeks into my first 12, I am happy to report that I have lost 1% body fat. That means I am close to my 2% goal. This is very encouraging to me! How have I gotten there? A relentless focus on diet and working out. In week five, I joined a CrossFit gym and will see how that impacts my fitness goals.

Write my first book for education

Well, I think it worked because you are reading this right now! I have not checked since week three, but at that point I had written 1/4 of my goal (25 of 100 topics) and I had written 10,000 words. Of course, at that time we are talking about my first draft. I have no idea how many words or topics will be included in the final edition. My goal was to write on two topics per day; I had generated a list of 100 topics prior to writing. For the first 22 days, I wrote on two topics each day. Then, I hit a bit of a slump and stopped writing for five days. Currently, I am on a nine-day streak.

Here were my results:

1. Added 12 mastermind clients.
2. Lost 3.5% body fat.
3. Wrote the first draft of this book.

Two things I learned from these 12 weeks:

- The system works.
- I truly believe that all of us have greatness within us.

What we lack are systems, mental models, and the community in which to make our dreams come into reality. The system I have for you will take care of that. Once I had the system, my productivity exponentially increased. So much so that my wife, Miriam, asked me to teach her.

You know it's a proven system when your partner says, "Teach me what you are doing I want to be as productive as you!" Wouldn't that be pretty cool? What would change at your job or at home if you accomplished in a quarter what it takes most people a year to do?

Measure Everything that Counts

Have you ever heard the phrase, "What gets measured gets done"? It is up for debate who coined it, but I like it. The phrase captures an important key to success. Measuring or having a system for "keeping score" shows an organization's priorities.

Just like in sports, there are winners and losers in any project, initiative, etc. Actually, there are only wins for those that learn from mistakes. The big idea I really want you to understand is that you need a system to measure what matters to you and your organization.

Because I have a system for measuring what matters, I have accomplished all of the goals I previously mentioned and more.

I kept my goals to no more than three and rigorously evaluated my performance toward these goals on a daily, weekly, and quarterly basis. I teach this system in my productivity course. Below are four ways to measure your goals:

Goal-crusher Template

The template is a turn-key solution for being more productive. All you need to do is choose between one and three goals that you would like to accomplish in the next 12 weeks. From there, you backward map. What needs to happen on a weekly basis, and what would that look like each day? Next you keep score and generate some major momentum toward accomplishing more than you ever have! I *guarantee* if you implement the system I teach, you will accomplish more in 12 weeks than most people do in 12 months. If I could guarantee your success and hand you the keys to being productive, what dreams would you chase after? I teach an effective system in my Goal-Crusher Course. I have also recorded a free webinar that will illustrate the lies that you believe about productivity and give you three mindset shifts that will absolutely change how you approach your work.

SMART Goals

SMART goals are popular, and I have used them with PLC teams and other school teams to accomplish great work. SMART stands for:

- Specific (They define all the key players, what they are doing, by when, and how.)
- Measurable (How will you know success has been reached?)
- Achievable (Is the goal realistic . . . is this pushing people to do their best without overwhelming them?)
- Results-Focused (What are the lag indicators . . . what will the output be after achieving the goal?)
- Time-bound (When will this project conclude?)

An example: By November 1st, 2017, all students in AP US History will use Cornell notes to synthesize readings and lectures from the course.

- Specific = all students in AP US
- Measurable = all students will use Cornell Notes
- Achievable = yes, given the correct incentives and support within class
- Results-Focused = Cornell notes
- Time-bound = November 1st, 2017

Learning Cycles

Learning Cycles are a school-wide focus after a Problem of Practice (POP). These can range from simple (all teachers will write the objective on the board) to more complex (all teachers will ask higher order questions using Bloom's taxonomy). To measure the POP during a learning cycle, the leadership team should choose not only the POP, but also how long they will measure results. Typically, this can be over a nine-week grading period. The learning cycle begins collecting baseline data. So in this example, let's say that we are going to measure if teachers are writing objectives on the board. A team would visit each classroom throughout a few-days-long period.

We used to give the schedule out ahead of time to encourage transparency. Then the team would collect data and report to the staff the baseline performance percentage. After that, teachers would have a few weeks of "safe practice" before another round of data collection occurred.

I suggest collecting data midway through the learning cycle and then at the end of the cycle. At each point, the staff should be aware and even discuss the results. Because support and PD is given throughout the cycle, you should see an improvement on a given POP chosen by the school. If you do see progress, it is now time to celebrate! If you do not see progress, it is time to explore why and regroup.

Life Plan

I teach this as a bonus to my productivity course. But the main idea I want to share with you is three parts. For the major areas of your life you want to think about:

1. your current reality,
2. your desired future, and
3. a plan on how to bridge the gap between your reality and desired future

This should be a list of things you can do and measure along the way.

I teach this much more in depth in my productivity course. If you want to get serious about your future, this bonus content from the course is worth the price of admission alone.

Focus on a Few Things and Do Not Sweat the Rest

You cannot do everything (or be everything), but I want to focus on what we can do right now. It is possible that your boss has unrealistic expectations of what you can accomplish in a given year. And maybe it is their boss who is equally unrealistic and that gets kicked down the line to you (and then to your staff). Do not do it. Protect your people however you can. This will take relational capital and a savvy understanding of what is and is not under your control. Given an ideal situation, where you have autonomy to select your performance goals and major initiatives, I have very simple advice.

Do not overdo it.

Or stated positively, choose your goals wisely. I teach in my productivity course to select between one and three goals per given period (which for my students is 12 weeks).

As I stated previously, **"What gets measured gets done."** Equally important is the idea to focus on the few things that really matter and do not sweat the rest.

SO WHAT DO YOU FOCUS ON?

What does your expert knowledge of your community say is the one big thing that, if accomplished, will impact everything else? That is where you start. I call it the "Big Domino." If you focus on a giant domino that if pushed will have a positive ripple effect throughout the organization, that is where you start.

There are 1,000 things that can be done each day, and not all of them are important. A search on the internet estimates that the average adult makes 35,000 decisions a day. The key to winning from decision fatigue is to limit the number of decisions we do make then and have a system for choosing the most important.

HOW DO I DO THAT?

Using data and my gut, I choose my top three goals for the quarter (e.g. add 10 mastermind clients, lose 1–2% body fat, and write my first book). And even though I need to build two new websites, create a new virtual workshop for school leaders, and grow my small-business owner coaching practice, I am ignoring it until the next 12 weeks starts.

I know I am most productive during the morning, so I start my day with a win (making my bed) and then use the rest of the morning to focus on my personal and professional goals. By midday, I transition to less impactful tasks such as email and other daily actions I have to do to maintain my business but not necessarily grow it.

If you start each day with a win in the morning and then use your most productive time to work on your priorities, you are going to be extremely productive. It is not rocket science, but it is challenging to execute. Start with a small win, and keep the momentum going.

CHAPTER 12 NEXT STEPS

- ☐ Choose no more than three goals per quarter (two professional and one personal).

- ☐ Measure everything you do personally and professionally. This can be how many times you went to the gym this week or through a format like the learning cycle for your school.

- ☐ Consider SMART goals and how you can apply them personally and professionally.

CHAPTER THIRTEEN

Important to Success

Get Clear on Your Vision, Mission, and Values

Proverbs 29:18 states "Where there is no vision, people scatter." Some versions of this proverb illustrate that the impact can be even more devastating, "Where there is no vision, people perish."

My former pastor used to say that a leader's job is to move his people from "here" to "there." How do you do that?

- By honestly considering where the current state of affairs are for your organization, and
- By painting such a compelling vision of the future that the current state of affairs seems undesirable.

The people will want to move.

The vision of an organization is where you are going, where you are headed. It should be exciting and persuasive while your staff should understand the exact target you are shooting for.

I help leaders create compelling vision stories that they weave into every communication regarding the organization.

The mission is how you operate each day and your core values reflect what your organization does better than anyone else.

In fact, Patrick Lencioni says that an organization is willing to be punished for living out their core values.

The CEO of Southwest Airlines once received a letter of complaint from a customer. At Southwest, they value humor and having fun. This value comes to life the second the airplane staff gets on the PA to talk to travelers; they are hilarious.

Well, the letter sent to the CEO did not find their behavior so funny and thought they should take safety a little more serious (the opposite of what Southwest values . . . they obviously value safety and take it seriously, but the staff discusses it in humorous ways).

So the CEO had a choice to make on his response.

He wrote, "You'll be missed."

That is an example of a company willing to get punished for their core values.

When designing vision, mission, and values, it has been my experience that schools often get this wrong by having too many voices at the table.

Raise your hand if you ever created your school's vision, mission, and values as an entire staff.

How many days did that take? How many people were truly invested in the process? Should everyone be included in this process?

No.

It is okay to set the vision, mission, and values of an organization as a leader. In fact, you were hired to do just that—tell your organization where it is going.

I am a proponent of considering your people's perspectives when forming the direction and goals of your organization. However, slugging through this process with the entire staff is a terrible waste of time. Step up and set the tone for your people.

Align the Personal and Professional

One thing professionals do better than amateurs is aligning their personal and professional visions. It is a myth that you should keep them separate. It is ridiculous to even try. When I reflect on the leaders I had the hardest time connecting to, the major barrier is they seemed a little less human.

They were all business. Are you?

We are complex creatures. What happens at home impacts our work and vice versa.

Amateurs live separate lives while professionals live a rich, integrated life where the personal and professional merge.

I will continue to promote balance as a major part of self-care. This is great leadership because you cannot give if your own tank is on empty.

When a personal and professional vision align, a powerful relationship is formed that drives momentum at work and at home. A leader can fire on all cylinders because she is living her passion. Nothing can stop her. The goals she pursues are relevant and meaningful. Therefore, the goals are actionable and have a greater likelihood of being accomplished. When personal and professional vision align, something powerful happens as a result.

Accountability = Ownership

In *The 12 Week Year*, the author Brian Moran argues that accountability = self ownership. He uses an interesting illustration to prove his point. **"You can hold a baby ... you can hold a bag of groceries ... but you can't hold someone accountable."**

Managers love to hide behind the idea of holding people "accountable" through power and intimidation. I agree with Moran, true accountability comes from within. I get things done and follow through on my word because it matters to me.

As a leader, you have to go a level or two deeper with your thinking. Effective leaders understand what inspires, motivates, and drives their people to their best work.

Focus on Strengths, not Weaknesses

I believe that focusing on your strengths is the single best choice a leader can make to move from good to great. Trying to correct weaknesses is not only a waste of time; it also has the potential to decrease our motivation and lower our confidence.

By focusing on our strengths as leaders, the opposite is true. Momentum is generated, and confidence is built. If we focus on strengths, that means we have very clear vulnerabilities. Instead of wasting time trying to change weaknesses from a "D" to a "C" grade performance, we should hire "A" players that complement our own skill set.

Our ego improves because if we are clear on what our strengths and weaknesses are, we are less likely to believe that we can do everything on our own and better than everyone else in the organization.

By adding diversity to our team in terms of strengths-based skills, we create a super team, like the Avengers, but for school leadership. However, this only happens for leaders courageous enough to identify their strengths *and* their weaknesses.

> Great leaders know they can accomplish more by concentrating on their strengths—rather than always correcting their weakness.
>
> —LOLLY DASKALL

Why waste time trying to improve areas of your life you don't even enjoy? Stay in a "flow" state and focus on your strengths. Develop that to Hollywood status and share this strength with the world. By narrowing your focus, not only will you have a greater impact, you will also be a lot happier.

Remember Michael Jordan playing baseball? Yeah, I barely do, and I only remember because I lived in Chicago and was a White Sox fan. I am glad that he returned to basketball. That was his gift to the world. What will be yours?

> Strengths are not activities you're good at; they're activities that strengthen you. A strength is an activity that before you're doing it you look forward to doing it; while you're doing it, time goes by quickly and you can concentrate; after you've done it, it seems to fulfill a need of yours.
>
> —MARCUS BUCKINGHAM

Know Your People

In the last topic, we explored focusing on strengths rather than weaknesses. Do this for your people, too.

One of the first things I did as principal was ask my awesome staff to take a StrengthsFinder personal assessment. The results were very interesting, which you can see in the following chart:

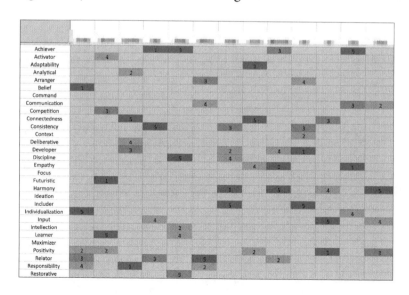

This data showed me my people's "narrow brilliance." The result was that I could use this information to make sure people were operating in their strengths based on their role.

Using a DISC profile can also be a powerful tool to investigate people's strengths. Knowing the DISC profile of your staff will help you understand how to communicate effectively with your staff, but also you will have a sense of their personality.

Are they more active (Ds & Is) or are they more passive (Ss & Cs). Armed with this data, you may have a better idea of what teams an individual should serve on and maybe where they can do their best work.

Even if you do not want to do a personality assessment, a leader can use observational data to place people in their strengths. Watch body language and listen for emotion and how people describe different aspects of the organization. If there is passion in the voice, put them on that project! Are they asleep at the meeting? Get them a nap pod or put them somewhere that excites them.

I can already hear the haters, "I hired her to do a job. They just need to do it."

Well, yes . . . and no.

I believe it is a leader's moral responsibility to place people in an area where they can add the most value and thrive. If you are ignoring people's talents, desires, and dreams, you have made a huge mistake. People are not replaceable parts within your organization. See them as the wonderful creations they are and get creative on how best to use their talents.

Push Up the Timeline

> Fortune favors the bold.
> —JOHN LEE DUMAS

What stops you from pulling the trigger? What obstacles, challenges, and barriers (real and perceived) get in your way?

I think many of us face real barriers that are physical.

Maybe it is the boss that does not get your new initiative and the direction you are headed. Can you communicate in a better way that she will understand? Did you try that and still face her resistance? Some people will just never support you. Your time is limited there. Move forward anyway, and make whatever impact you can during your time.

Maybe you face the challenge of staff or community buy-in. Be inspiring. Be memorable. And be a person of the people.

Sure, you have bold visions to run after, but they do not matter unless others care about the same dream.

Make it their dream too.

Ask what dreams they have and then package it in a way (especially using their own words) that it seems relatable . . . their idea even. Then serve. Serve your community the best idea you have and help them see the value in the direction you are going and how that benefits them all.

Maybe the challenge is data, the plan, and the need for perfection. Analysis paralysis is very real. We can get lost in our heads and continue to frame and work on the perfect plan while the timing is missed and the opportunity ship sails.

But maybe your main challenge is yourself. The reptilian brain is turned on in its effort to protect you. "Don't jump," it says, and you heed its warning missing out on the expiration of acting on the dream, executing, and changing lives for the better.

When you face obstacles, whether they are real or perceived, in our head they slow us down.

The antidote is to jump all-in.

Push up the timeline and *make it happen*.

Your idea might not be perfect, but you can improve on it later.

You will not accomplish anything without taking that first step. Go!

Loose–Tight

Rick and Becky DuFour are known for their work establishing the idea of Professional Learning Communities at Work.

This is an interesting way to organize schools so that they are much more responsive to students' needs, but in terms of this chapter Rick and Becky offered a helpful insight: Loose vs. Tight.

Another way leaders can get out of the way of creativity and innovation is by clearly defining their loose and tight rules.

Tight rules are nonnegotiable and establish what must be done no matter what.

Loose rules allow the practitioner on the ground to make decisions (because she is a professional) on how to play within the boundaries agreed upon. A Loose–Tight system works for everyone involved because it gives a leader a sense of peace knowing that the agenda moves forward while giving autonomy to the professionals that actually make the dream come true.

In this type of system, ideas flow like water.

Of course, if an idea does not work the data should support this and ideas can then be revised and executed.

In the context of a Professional Learning Community, an example of tight rules would be: all teachers will create common assessments, meet regularly to analyze data, and design interventions in response to the data. These are the broad and tight system set up for teachers to play within.

Loose rules: how teachers design the common assessments, how they meet to discuss/analyze data, and how they design and implement interventions. These are up to their professional creativity.

Clouds and Dirt

I did not come up with this idea. Gary Vee did. I encourage the reader to search his YouTube channel for the topic "Clouds and Dirt."

The idea is simple but often overlooked by leaders.

Clouds represent the vision. The BHAGs (Big Hairy Audacious Goals) that we have. The could answer the question, "Where do we want to be in three years, five years, 10 years, etc.?" Clouds are strategic.

The dirt is the day-to-day tactics that matter. Dirt is operational.

Action-oriented. Tactical. Without dirt, nothing gets done. Buildings do not open. Classes are not taught. Students do not graduate.

Dirt often dominates the school leader's thinking. When something urgent pops up, the school leader runs off to solve that problem. The emails that pile up and the observations (and feedback) that need to be completed. Dirt is important, but dirt does not inspire, grow, or innovate. Without the clouds, schools will become irrelevant and dare I say that many of them already have died a dirt death?

Clouds inspire us to the next level. They are in the sky for a reason. This is where our gaze turns for inspiration. I used to love reading poetry out on the grass of the quad at the University of Illinois. Propped up against a tree, I would read Langston Hughes or William Carlos Williams and then gaze up to the sky contemplating life. What is the meaning of it all? Where am I going next? How did I want to use my gifts and talents to impact the world? Be careful, though; live only in the clouds and you will die only having accomplished dreaming big dreams while never taking action. This temptation is very real as well. It is easier to think and dream and avoid acting. There is safety there. No risk (nor reward). You will not strike out if you never step up to the plate.

To be effective, a school leader needs her eyes on the clouds at all times while she stands firmly planted in the dirt. Both are needed to be great.

Believe—You Get What You Ask For

I completed an online workshop with Seth Godin that deeply moved me in many ways. Here is one quote that I never will forget. It shook me and has inspired me to be better ever since. I hope it has the same effect on you:

> You get the culture you deserve.
> —SETH GODIN

[INSERT CLASSICAL MUSIC AND DRAMATIC PAUSE]

Ouch.

As I said, this quote shook me because it challenged me to really take ownership over my leadership. The culture that I saw every day was the exact culture I deserved.

All the good parts . . . I influenced that, but all the bad parts . . . that was me too. That quote exposed me.

Not that I was hiding in my office all day without leading. This quote increased my self-accountability in a way that few other words could. I had to step up my game.

The funny thing about culture is that it has so much to do with what we expect. Unpacking Seth's quote makes me think that culture is a result of actions (deposits into the culture) we make over time.

And what guides those actions? Our beliefs, mindsets, and conscious or unconscious biases. I have found through experience that people, both kids and adults, give you exactly what you expect 99% of the time. I have to leave at least 1% out there for the crazy that do not respond to anything that works for everyone else. They seem to belong to a whole other universe!

Taking the crazies out of the picture, then, I believe that people give you what you expect 100% of the time. I have seen this most dramatically as a teacher. The same students, misfits my colleagues might call them, would perform extremely well for me while in other classes they struggled as if they were another human being altogether.

Why is that? Teacher expectations were incongruent. Respect was demanded rather than given. Relationships remained unnurtured. While I expected and demanded success a peer may think much less of the same students.

I experienced this as a school leader. Working for the absolute worst boss I have ever experienced, I saw my own performance decline. Because of an emotionally abusive environment, I found myself making mistakes that I have never made in my life. I would write emails (that she had to read and approve of course . . . micromanagement at its finest!) and they would contain factual errors (I would use the wrong teacher's name for instance). This was crazy to me. Once removed from the environment and with plenty of time to detox, I was able to reflect on why this occurred.

She expected me to fail. As a result, I could never succeed in that environment. "You get the culture you deserve."

Four Agreements

A *big* shout out to Jimmy Casas, who recommended the book *The Four Agreements: A Practical Guide to Personal Freedom* by Don Miguel Ruiz to me. This was a spiritual experience as I listened to the story via Audible.

I am committed to self exploration, growth, and personal mastery. This is a challenging and fantastic book if this theme appeals to you as well. Before I summarize the Four Agreements, I want to state a foundational belief that I have about leadership.

"You can only lead others at a high level after you have learned how to lead yourself."

The metaphor I like to use here is the image of a cup. As a leader we want to be full to the point of "overflowing." When our cup is overflowing we have plenty to give others. If our cup is only half full or worse, empty, there is nothing to give. What do you need to do each day to take care of yourself? What activities give you life and restoration?

For me, I am filled up when I can:

- spend time in solitude (reading, writing, meditating, praying, and/or listening to music)
- work out
- play guitar
- spend time outside
- go for a walk with Miriam or sit and converse with her

If I take time to do these things that make me happy, I am in a much better place to give to others. When I take care of myself I am successful because, then, and only then, can I truly serve as I have been called to do as a leader.

After you begin a journey of self-care, then consider committing to the Four Agreements as presented by Don Miguel Ruiz:

1. BE IMPECCABLE WITH YOUR WORD:

Your words mean everything. Do what you say, and say what you do. Be positive in your speech.

> Kind words are like honey—
> sweet to the soul
> and healthy for the body.
>
> —PROVERBS 16:24 (NLT)

Avoid negative talk about yourself and others. Words are powerful. Always use them for good.

2. DO NOT TAKE ANYTHING PERSONALLY.

This is particularly tough for me. As a leader, we each get to field all the complaints that our community has. As a podcaster, I put myself out there. My goal is to be authentic: to show both my big wins and colossal failures. As the show has grown, I have started to attract some "trolls."

This is very difficult to not take personally.

The key here is to understand that we never have the full story. The iceberg metaphor is appropriate here. Below the surface of the water is the majority of the iceberg, but we do not see it above the water. Just like the iceberg, our staff and students bring a variety of experiences to school each day that we may or may not be aware of. These experiences greatly impact the choices each human makes. If someone is frustrated with you, get curious, and avoid taking it personally.

3. DO NOT MAKE ASSUMPTIONS.

Above, I stated to get curious if someone seems to be "attacking" you. Curiosity is rooted in asking questions.

Let's say a coworker is having a bad day. Instead of taking it personally try asking, "Hey, Melissa, it seems like you are distracted and impatient today. Am I reading this right? Is everything okay?"

Find the courage to ask questions and to express what you really desire. By actively listening and truly trying to understand you can turn enemies into evangelists. It is hard to oppose someone who really "gets" you.

4. ALWAYS DO YOUR BEST.

Easy to say and hard to do. By agreeing with excellence, you agree with success and health. Do not focus on the outcomes; rather, focus on your effort and doing your personal best.

That is why lead and lag indicators are so important. The lag indicator will always occur, and when it does, it is too late, for better or worse. You want to lose weight in time for the beach. When summer arrives, it is too late. If you measure lead indicators on the way to a summer goal (measuring food, amount of time you spend in the gym, avoiding sugar, etc.), you are more likely to experience the outcome you desire. That is how you focus on effort.

> It's far better when doing good work is sufficient . . . the less attached we are to outcomes the better. When fulfilling our own standards is what fills us with pride and self respect. When the effort—not the results, good or bad—is enough.
>
> —RYAN HOLIDAY

What Helps People Succeed?

Have you read *Drive* yet by Daniel Pink? This book had me uttering to myself, "Yes, yes, yes!"

The basic premise is that how we build our organizations to motivate does not reflect what science reveals about what truly motivates us.

Well, that is a problem!

According to Pink, there are three principles leaders need to pay attention to: autonomy, mastery, and purpose.

AUTONOMY:

We do not need a boss, nor do we like a boss telling us what to do. As I have stated before, the leader's main job is to cast a compelling vision, clearly articulate the organization's values, remove barriers, and provide support for staff as they grow in competence. A leader's job is to connect people's passion to the task at hand.

If the staff is clear about where the organization is going and how the organization behaves, get the heck out of the way! If the work is connected to people's underlying passions, then they will get emotional reward from their work (and will not need you to motivate them).

Let your people do their work. Provide time and resources they need. Help people connect their passion to their work. Give coaching where applicable (which moves us into the next idea of Pink's motivation) . . .

MASTERY:

People want to know that the work they do matters and that they are competent performers.

Coaching provides a nonthreatening way to provide feedback on how to improve. In many of our lives, a coach had tremendous impact in our lives. Use this type of posture while leading, and people will love you.

Find out what your people's desires and dreams are both personally and professionally. Notice. Write them down. Ask them about their goals. Provide them help to master them.

Zig Ziglar said you can have anything in this world (riches) as long as you help enough people to get what they want. As school leaders, we are not going to accumulate a bunch of riches, but the idea works for us as well. We can garner great influence just as long as we help everyone in our organization get what they want.

PURPOSE:

No organization has as natural and easy a job as a school to provide purpose for their employees. It is intrinsic to the DNA of a school. Every day we come to work and serve kids, we say, "Yes, I want to be a part of something bigger than myself."

As school leader, you are Chief Story Officer. Constantly remind your staff about your school's *Why*. Tell stories and retell the same stories until they become a part of the organization's fabric and lore. They should illustrate your organization's value and pull at the your staff's hearts.

Remind them that they have an incredible opportunity to make a difference in a kid's life today and every day of the school year.

CHAPTER 13 NEXT STEPS

☐ Get clear on your vision, mission, and core values. There is plenty of information available online, but if I can help let me know.

☐ In my opinion, it is a mistake to be "all business." Do not separate the personal and professional. People want authenticity, connection, and community. Show up at work by bringing your personal *and* professional personas.

☐ Add diversity to your team—not only through gender, race, religion, sexual orientation, etc., but also by adding people whose strengths bolster your weaknesses. Your organization cannot truly be great if everyone thinks like you!

☐ Reflect on where you are dragging your feet. Remember that "Fortune favors the bold." Take action and adjust/iterate where needed. You miss 100% of the shots you never take.

☐ Consider what rejuvenates you. When planning your week, block out time for yourself and family first. Then schedule professional events around your life. Believe me, if you do not prioritize your life, no one will.

PART TWO: CHANGING SCHOOLS

CHAPTER FOURTEEN

Changing the Structure

SHOULDN'T SCHOOL BE FUN? As educators, we are lucky. We work with the world's most important resource and have the best job on Earth. Where else do you get instant feedback that "showing up" today mattered? Kids are brutally honest . . .

KID: What is that large bump on your forehead, Mr. Bauer? Did you get bit by a spider?

ME: That is a pimple (thinking, *Thanks for pointing it out, kiddo!*)

Too often, educators walk around the halls of a school with a permanent scowl on their face. Are these educators allergic to smiles and innovation . . . maybe even children too? They forgot the answer to "*Why school?*" is that we can change the world as educators.

What an opportunity!

What other industry has the unique gift of impacting the world in that way, day in and day out? This premise should leave every educator with a smile on her face. Every day, we impact lives.

This should be fun!

My earliest memory of school was walking to kindergarten. My teacher's name was Mrs. Sunshine, a perfect name for a kindergarten teacher at Jane Addams Elementary School in Palatine, IL. I do not remember what I learned, but I do remember that I liked show-and-tell and my reading buddy.

Show-and-Tell

I loved show-and-tell because it gave me a platform to express myself. Now I do it publicly though a podcast and blog, but back in the early '80s, I presented my pet turtle or one of my authentic German hand-crafted nutcrackers my mom bought me each Christmas.

Show-and-tell resonated with me because it was authentic and I got to speak about things I cared about.

How often do we give this opportunity to kids nowadays? Do we allow them to explore topics of their interest and present? Do we ask modern-day students to solve interesting problems that are not found in a textbook?

Reading Buddy

Mentors are important. I do not remember my 4th grade mentor's name, but I remember loving the time he would spend reading to me or going on field trips and falling asleep on his shoulder riding back to school on the bus.

Mentors are important because they show us where we can go. How often do we connect our kids to older mentors to unlock future possibilities for younger students? Plus, mentorship is a gift to the mentor. In this relationship, mentors often experience deep levels of satisfaction by giving back and teaching others.

Elementary School and High School

At this level, I have many positive memories. The positive memories all revolve around making friends or "the awakening" that accompanies puberty and the realization that I really liked girls. Most days were happy with the opportunity to socialize. And for me, few, very few memories are actually connected to learning.

In the 4th grade, I remember Jeff Larson smashing a banana on Mrs. K's desk during lunch. In those days, we ate our lunch in our classroom with no supervision. I guess smashed bananas are sometimes the result, and the class erupted in laughter. That made Jeff a legend, and he has been smashing bananas ever since!

In 5th grade, I remember solving a critical thinking mystery that Mrs. R read to the class. The story involved a crime and someone writing a letter supposedly in a car (along a bumpy ride). I noticed that the writing was impeccable and therefore, could not have been written during a bumpy car ride! The person on trial was obviously lying and I was first to catch it. I felt pretty smart!

In 6th grade, I loved taking a creative writing class. We made our own books of poetry (which I still have to this day). I wrote poems about baseball, a limerick that vilified my sister, and a haiku about crushing a fly. This was really Shakespearean stuff!

In 7th grade, I took an advanced math class with 8th graders. I learned how to solve equations, but more importantly, I stared at two incredibly cute red-headed cousins, dressed in the white shirt and plaid skirt combo famous in parochial schools.

I do not remember learning much in 8th grade or high school. I remember another creative writing course I took and the time I told Mr. R, my Geology teacher, that I had to save a Girl Scout troop from a burning house on my way to school, and that is why I was late to class. He laughed and did not give me a tardy that day. Oh . . . and when we dissected pigs, I had the bright idea of throwing the nose at Lisa because she was cute.

My sophomore year, I made a mixtape for Geometry class with my friend, Chet. We sang about rhombi and angles. We created Christmas songs infused with geometric principles accompanied by some incredible Casio keyboard melodies. We sang about Mrs. H, recently engaged, and how we wanted her to leave her fiancé for us. Embarrassing. Slightly inappropriate. And wildly fun. Mrs. H was hot.

I do not remember any tests from class.

College

It was not until college that I really remember learning. I suppose that is because as a college student I had great autonomy in choosing what I learned about—whether that was Japanese Culture, African-American Literature, Shakespeare, Astrology, or Educational Psychology.

Again, social aspects of college bring back many fond memories, but I loved researching and writing on topics that explored literature or helped me to form my philosophy of education.

In college, I learned that I sucked at writing—thanks, high school! My first grade on a paper was an F. Thankfully, I received feedback on how I could improve and finally, I started to write somewhat competently.

I switched from wanting to teach math (and wear plaid button-down shirts complete with pocket protectors and thick-rimmed glasses) to wanting to teach English. I had a blind professor who taught a poetry class. He loved a reading and interpretation I did of an Edgar Allen Poe poem. This encouragement unlocked my desire to teach English with one affirming remark and changed the trajectory of my life. And the girls studying English were very cute. Much cuter than the guys who studied math. Smashing bananas is fun. Meeting girls is better.

Honing our voice through writing about topics important to us is great. School should be fun.

What Happened to Recess?

Not only should school be fun, it should also allow kids to be active. In the US, a focus on testing results in two subjects that are quick to be cut:

1. Recess
2. The arts

I needed recess throughout elementary school. When I worked at Memorial Middle School as principal, the students did not have recess. Fortunately, the APs found a way to let kids out just a little early from lunch each day so they could play in the courtyard. With only 10 minutes of free time, kids would run like wild animals playing tag and other types of games. They needed a physical outlet to get the energy out. Once a quarter, we also had a walk-the-track event to prioritize movement and healthy lifestyle choices. It never surprised me when a good portion of the students would literally run the entire 26-minute "walking" period. Kids are fat. They are fat because they lack access to high quality, nutrient-rich food, and they lack opportunities to exercise.

Why aren't we providing this for our students regularly?

Contrast that with kids in Belgium. I have lived here for about a month at the time of this writing, and the thing I quickly noticed . . . kids are not fat here! It probably helps that they walk and cycle everywhere. Fitness is built into the lifestyle.

It does not matter what country you live in. Fitness benefits human beings, and we should prioritize it in schools.

In the podcast, *School of Greatness*, Lewis Howes and Dr. Michael Gervais unpack high performance. The research found students who participate in sports and the arts develop more grit as adults. So why do we cut these programs from our schools?

All throughout my educational career not only did I participate in sports, I also played the alto saxophone, sang in the choir, and performed in musicals.

The arts taught me about beauty, expression, and critical thinking. These were easily my favorite classes because they were both highly social and highly enjoyable. They were rewarding because I could clearly see the fruit of my labor. And the final product . . . the performance . . . was the best part.

Whether I was leading the band and shaking my hips as the drum major or dancing and singing in *The Music Man*, I loved to perform.

Guess where I come up with the majority of my best ideas for BLBS?

In the gym or while playing my guitar!

Shoot . . . I still remember coming up with the idea of starting the blog and podcast while lifting heavy weights at an FFC in Chicago.

Great ideas are created when people unwind and blow off steam. Our brains need that time to solve complex problems while our bodies are active doing something else. On the playground and the stage, I learned valuable lessons like teamwork, navigating jerks, expression, critical thinking, and how to talk to girls.

Recess and the arts should be the last thing to be cut.

Play

I know Disney thinks that it is "the happiest place on Earth," but in my opinion, the happiest place should really be school. It is not the Disney brand that makes it the happiest place; it is the imagination of the kids. Where Disney excels is that they make the environment ripe for imagination to grow, explore, and play.

Kids are experts at that.

So why do schools shut down and shut out the magic our children bring to us each day? How could our schools be more like Disney? I am not proposing that we need to dress up in mouse and princess costumes (but that would be fun), but I am pushing school leaders to think about environment.

How can we make schools more . . .

- Magical?
- Welcoming?
- Fun?
- Experiential?
- Delivering some type of "Wow" experience that kids can't wait to tell their parents?

How do we do this? I have many ideas. What I will do is give you 10 (Thanks, James Altucher). Come up with your own list with your leadership team, staff, and community. The trick is *do not evaluate* a single idea. Brainstorm until your nugget is out of juice and you are mentally exhausted. Most of the ideas might be complete garbage, but what if one idea changes the landscape of education in your school, district, state, country, or the world?

10 Ways to Incorporate More Play and Magic into School

1. A 15-minute recess after every class.
2. One morning class that infuses all the core subjects and arts into a single class. The afternoon is for playing, independent projects, and team building (and a nap).
3. Dress up like my new friend Andy Jacks. He frequently dresses as a banana or gorilla to create a fun atmosphere for his kids and staff.
4. Build some type of ride or game at your school for kids to play before and after school, during lunch, and passing periods. Why not? Ryan Jackson and his students built an escape room.
5. Create one class called "Play." Put one smart adult that will just resource kids, get out of the way, and play with students.
6. Add a bunch of live animals to the school. Let them roam the halls and classes. Let the kids take care of them. See what happens.
7. Start every day with an all-school assembly + dance-off between students and staff.
8. Protect the arts, clubs, and sports at your school.
9. When anyone, a kid or an adult, is taking themselves too seriously, throw a pie in their face.
10. Create a nickname for every student and staff member and use it lovingly.

(BONUS IDEA) Write a movie/play/musical, and give everybody a part in the school. Then film it/present it each year. School, not Disney, should be the happiest place on Earth.

Gamification

Why are games on our smart devices or gaming systems so addictive? We can clearly see our progress and celebrate our results! Each time we beat a level, save a princess, or reach a high score, we earn a badge. We become more powerful and get more gamer "clout." Our rank goes up, and so does our prestige.

How could we award badges to both our students and staff members? Would this motivate them to achieve at even higher rates? I believe it would.

Throw Out Tradition

Tradition stinks. It keeps us where we are safe and allows us to color within the lines, but it never pushes us to innovation or creativity. We can die with tradition. It is like a warm blanket.

Traditional schools are not serving students to the best of their ability. Students are growing disconnected and looking to learn elsewhere.

What do we need to rethink?

1. class structure
2. bell schedule
3. seat time
4. rows
5. etc.

Class Structure

Classes are taught in isolation, but why? Science is not just science and English is not just literature or grammar. As an adult, we see the connections between the disciplines, yet we tend to teach them in isolation. It is crazy. I would love to see schools move toward projects or themed days, weeks, and months. Schools should be giving students interesting problems to solve and then teaching the disciplines through these projects.

Bell Schedule

Classes one through eight meet for 40–45 minutes Monday through Friday. This is a misrepresentation of reality.

I do not just work for 40 minutes and then shut things down to work on the next task. A bell does not ring telling me to move forward no matter where I am at in a project.

Take this book for example. It was written in eight weeks (as part of my 12-week goal). I wrote two topics a day, every day, for eight weeks.

First draft done. Then I edited and shipped. It took 12 weeks to write this book, and I wrote two topics a day. This might take 20 minutes or four hours. No bells and no whistles. I wrote until I accomplished my goal and then I moved on. With intense focus, I was able to accomplish this. Sometimes it took me 40 minutes to just warm up! Ding! Next class . . .

Seat Time

If I can learn to code a website in one month, why would I take a two-year program to get "certified" or "graduate" to create websites? We stifle growth and curiosity by creating artificial barriers to students' success. The key is mastery. Students should work until they master content and then move on.

This takes fluidity and creativity on our part as school leaders, but it would be interesting to see how education would transform if we moved to this kind of system. Need a starting point? Check out Summit Learning online.

Rows

Compliance. Order. A teacher's best friend. I like messy and collaborative. Do you value this at your school?

Teach kids how to collaborate appropriately. Buy some great school furniture that promotes collaboration and see what the kids come up with next.

Rows should be banished.

Turn the Bells Off and Restructure the Day

I know there are law and state mandates and policy and blah blah blah. Turn that off for a moment. Stop following directions. Be original. What would happen to school if we turned the bells off? Why do they exist anyway? Do we really need to a signal of when to get out of our seats, to go to lunch, to go home and pat ourselves on the back for a job well done.

I love how we say in schools, "That is not how the real world works." We use this phrase to scare and intimidate (a whole other topic for a book) students into being more compliant:

- To follow the rules . . .
- To be quiet . . .
- Stand straight in line . . .
- And enjoy a 20-minute lunch (and no recess).

Man, when you think about it that way, school sucks! Let's unplug. Let's turn the bells off.

Why? Well, because that is how the real world works . . . In the real world:

- You work until the job is done.
- You solve interesting problems.
- You manage multiple projects.
- The market, the investors, or the community evaluates your performance.

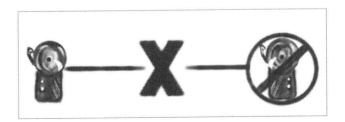

Traditional School with Bells   **Modern School Without Bells**

Shoot for the X!

Imagine a school where students were allowed to not only take classes they were interested in learning the topics, but they did not have a bell that ushered them onto the next class and then the next . . .

With my mastermind, we constantly talk about engaging in "Deep work" and producing work that is meaningful. The irony, how do eight 40–45 minute blocks allow our students to do the same?

CHAPTER 14 NEXT STEPS

☐ Generate a list of 10 ideas that would make your school more fun (or steal mine). Choose one item on the list. Take action. Your community will love you for it! Protect recess, the arts, and sports. You will build grittier, more well-rounded human beings as a result.

CHAPTER FIFTEEN

Old School vs. New School

Tough Choices

Educators, you have a choice. Do you teach to the test, or help kids develop a love for learning?

Is this an "either or" question or "both and"? At least in America, we love the test. From what I understand from my friend Clayton, Australia loves the test too, but this is not necessarily true for the rest of the world.

What are the results of focusing on preparing kids for a test?

While I was a principal in Texas I read an article, "I Can't Answer These Texas Standardized Test Questions About My Own Poem." The title pretty much explains it all. Poet Sara Holbrook tried to answer questions on the Texas standardized test (STAAR) about a poem she authored, and she failed!

Testing is done by for-profit entities and makes big bucks each year. Politicians are happy to use these results to get elected, and the government can hide behind the results to justify its investment in education.

In 2015, the US spent 54% of it is discretionary funding on the military ($598.5 billion) compared to 6% on education ($70 billion). I have been told in life and in business you can reveal a man's priorities by investigating how he invests his time and his money. It is clear what is prioritized in the US.

What is the cost of this prioritization?

I would argue the cost is the creation of a society less capable of critical thinking and less of a fostered love of learning. If this is true, then what kind of society are we producing?

I do not want to be all gloom and doom, but (re)pose the original question:

Do you teach to the test, or help kids develop a love for learning?

When I entered the field of education in 2001, I couldn't care less about test results. As I mentioned in an earlier chapter, leadership is about relationships and connection. I think education is about this, too.

By developing strong relationships with students, we can push them to take risks, encourage failure (and the learning it will produce), and inspire greatness and innovation. Through developing relationships, we fertilize the soil in which we can inspire a deep love for learning. Books congregate on shelves and whisper to me, "Continue to learn." I have a deep satisfaction in my life because I am a learner, not because I scored well on the ACT.

In third grade, Ms. Behrman shared with the class her passion for dinosaurs. The whole year, we studied all sorts of facts about dinosaurs culminating with a trip to the Field Museum in Chicago where we could view Sue, the museum's pride and joy. Sue is a full-scale T-Rex that towers over everyone in the lobby. I do not remember how I scored on any test in 3rd grade through college for that matter, but I do remember the passion that Mrs. B transferred to the entire class, and I thank her for that. I had dinosaur toys and dinosaur books. I could not get enough about dinosaurs, and although I do not read about them now, what Mrs. B taught me was a love of learning that continues to this day.

alienearbud

alienearbud Mrs. B, my 3rd grade teacher, retired Sunday after 35 years. 1987 & 25 years later

JUNE 4, 2012

Add a comment...

Familiar & Safe

Tradition. One of the deadliest phrases in the world is "We've always done it that way; it's tradition."

I dislike that phrase because it does not provide a solution to any of the problems we face in education. Things stay the same because they are familiar and safe, such as the class schedule and structure mentioned in Chapter 14. Somehow this is okay for schools. I am not sure how we have not changed that much in over a century. It is crazy if you think about it.

Imagine the first cell phone that was created when you were alive. Now imagine whatever latest model you are salivating for.

When I was a kid, a cell phone was literally a brick. It got very hot when you used it. The phone weighed a ton and you could only make calls (that were very expensive to make!).

Now the iPhone I have is so small and light, it literally flies out of my hand when I take it out of my pocket. It is also much more than a phone. The latest iPhone has more computing power than the first computers!

Here is a picture of a school in the US circa 1943.

And a pic of a modern-day classroom . . .

**"Student Lab Classroom Science Lesson Students"
by Max Pixel is licensed under CC 2.0.**

Sure, we have advanced in some ways, but when compared to how fast technology advances, I must ask, "Have schools really advanced at all?" Meanwhile, the curriculum, the cafeteria, and the classroom remain the same. What is the cost?

Disconnection.

Disillusion.

Dreams deferred.

Ineffective works because it is easy and safe. It is tradition. It's "the devil we know."

So why change it?

I think the status quo also exists because of another important reason.

People are blind to the credible alternatives that already exist and the pioneers blazing an exciting new frontier in education.

Kids do not even watch TV anymore. Celebrities to a modern middle-schooler are found on YouTube, Instagram, and Music.ly.

Yet schools stay the same and "teach" the same.

We need to change and change fast before we lose touch with our students completely.

Eleven Alternatives

So if tradition exists because it is familiar and safe, change is hard, and people are not aware of alternatives, let me offer a few.

I really enjoy consuming content by James Altucher. You should really check him out.

One of his mantras is to "Choose Yourself."

This might be the most powerful thing that I did in 2017.

Because I chose myself, you are reading this manifesto today, or maybe you have listened to me on the podcast, or perhaps have worked with me in a virtual leadership workshop or mastermind.

Since I chose myself, I have left behind the familiar and safe. I chose the unexpected, the daring, the risky.

It is scary.

And rewarding.

But back to James Altucher . . . in *Choose Yourself*, he shares this idea of "The Daily Practice." You should start it. Part of The Daily Practice is writing a list of 10 ideas a day.

Make your brain sweat. Stretch your critical thinking muscles.

So that is what this chapter is all about—a list of alternatives to the familiar and safe in education.

11 Alternatives to the Familiar & Safe in Education

1. Solve interesting problems through projects and writing. Abandon the standardized test.

2. Encourage college and yet do not encourage college. Debt is bad. Also, college is not for everybody. Sure, college is great for socialization and learning how to think, but can you learn that somewhere else? A kid can go into a trade and thrive from learning under an expert. Why not pursue that? He or she can build an online platform and personal brand and become a celebrity and make more money than I have in my entire career by following their passion. Why not encourage that?

3. Get rid of the eight class period day. Create schedules that are fluid and focus on students' passions. Let them learn important skills through what inspires them.

4. Offer flexible seating and standing options. Any class with desks in rows should be destroyed.

5. Burn textbooks that offer a biased view of history and reality. I was shocked to read an article in the *New York Times* in 2015 that highlighted a Texas textbook that described slaves as "workers." A whitewashed history that glosses over the horrors of slavery has no value and no place in schools. Read alternative histories like Howard Zinn. Question everything. Realistically reflect on the past to develop a well-rounded understanding of history so we can avoid the same mistakes.

6. Allow students to learn from anywhere. Create virtual-only schools with regular meet-ups.

7. Clearly identify capstone learning. Let students progress through it at their own pace. Forget about ages and grades as the only way to really progress through school.

8. Integrate schools.

9. Equally fund schools.

10. Celebrate kids every day for making awesome choices.

11. Stop punishing kids with detention and suspension as the only means of a "consequence." Look at the US penal system. Is it working? People learn from rehabilitation and better ways to solve problems. Detention does not teach a "bad" student that. Invest in restorative practices and consider using mindfulness as a way to reset kids. Create a school like Hi-Tech High. Connect with Kyle Wagner to learn how to be innovative in schools.

Bonus list:
10 People You Should Be Reading, Following, and Listening to for Inspiration

1. Seth Godin. Read the manifesto that inspired this one or check out this book, *Poke the Box* to challenge your thinking (@thisissethsblog).

2. James Altucher. He has a podcast, blog, and an inspiring book: *Choose Yourself* (@jaltucher).

3. Tim Ferriss. He interviews incredibly talented people on his podcast and will inspire you to be better (@tferriss).

4. Glenn Robbins. He is an All-Star Superintendent. If I still lived in the States, I would want to work in his district or connect on Twitter (@glennr1809).

5. Gary Vaynerchuck. You might not be starting a business as an educator, but the way Gary views technology can vastly improve how we implement it and how we connect with students (@garyvee).

6. Jennifer Abrams. She is a master of difficult conversations. This year, she is really intrigued by the idea of "Playing in the Deep End." I love it. She takes risks (@jenniferabrams).

7. Eric Barker. He writes the blog "Barking Up the Wrong Tree" and boils down interesting ideas into easily digestible nuggets of truth (@bakadesuyo).

8. Shane Farnam. Shane offers mental models to help you improve your critical thinking through his blog (@farnamstreet).

9. Ryan Jackson. This is my fiery friend in Tennessee. I admire what he does at #TheMount and the #UnderdogAdvocate brand he has built. Check out his blog and connect on Twitter (@ryanbjackson1).

10. Jeff Veal. He co-founded #leadupchat, the best chat for educators on Twitter (Saturdays 8:30 am CDT). Connect with Jeff on Twitter (@JHeffrey).

Inch Wide and a Mile Deep

This is the tension every educator must face. Do you try to appease the bureaucratic forces that design standards and curriculum maps, or do you go deep with your students? You cannot do both.

Local and statewide forces dictate what should be taught, and it has been documented that it is physically impossible to teach all the standards in one academic year. Yet each year, educators across the globe scurry to cover these standards at a breakneck pace despite if students are learning or not. "We must move on . . . we have more content to cover!" is a common cry heard in AP classes around the world. The problem with covering content is students never go deep with the content we claim to care about.

This is not just a problem on our students' end. As adults we do not learn that way, either. In my productivity course, I teach clients to pick between one and three goals. Never, ever do they pick more than three goals to accomplish over a three-month period.

Why?

Choosing more than three goals is unrealistic. You cannot actively pursue that many goals because your focus is spread too thin. It is easy to get overwhelmed with too much to do (or learn). So why do we do this to our students? This is a modern challenge of the school leader. For years, teachers have been pushed (and evaluated on) whether or not they prepared kids for the next year by "covering all the content."

Will you take a stand with me? It is going to require time, relationships, and trust. Do not use evaluations against teachers. Tell them and better yet, show them that you want them to take their time with content in order to go deep. This is the kind of learning that inspires. Demand that your teachers go an inch wide and a mile deep rather than an inch deep and a mile wide. It starts with you, but they can do it if you support them!

Stop Using PowerPoint Incorrectly

We are killing people with PowerPoint. It is lazy and toxic. According to Tim Pollard, author of *The Compelling Communicator*, PowerPoint and Keynote were not even designed for presentations. The default is slapping a bunch of text on 100 slides and then reading those same slides to the audience.

Kill me now. Please.

My interest in great presenting and the artful use of PowerPoint really began after seeing Seth Godin present at the Global Leadership Summit in 2011.

I already admired Seth because of his writing ability, but his presenting skills increased my respect to a whole new level. He skillfully used images and story throughout the presentation to emphasize the point he was trying to land.

I never forgot this strategy, and it has served me well ever since.

I investigated to see if he had ever written about it. Of course, he had, and you can read his ideas on "Really Bad PowerPoint" on his blog (and linked up in my resource accompaniment to this book). I will also summarize his key points below:

COMMUNICATION IS THE TRANSFER OF EMOTION.

Our job as presenters is to present with emotion why our topic matters and to help our audience adopt or understand our point of view. We have two sides of our brain. Using only facts and figures while ignoring the emotional side is a terrible mistake.

PRESENTERS MUST SELL.

If everyone believed what we did as a presenter, we wouldn't need to present, would we? You have to convince the audience that your topic matters.

FOUR COMPONENTS TO A GREAT PRESENTATION:

1. Use cue cards. Keep them in your hand and not on the screen as slides.
2. Use slides to reinforce your ideas (with emotion).
3. Create a written document to leave behind. That way people do not have to worry about notes and can focus on the emotional stories you share.
4. Create a feedback cycle. Whatever you present on, the audience should be urged to take action in some way, right then and there.

FIVE RULES FOR POWERPOINT:

1. Have six or fewer words to a slide.
2. Use professional photos.
3. Eliminate transitions.
4. Limit sound effects, and if you use them, avoid "stock" sounds. Use music to connect with people's emotions. I use epidemicsound.com to add music to my videos.
5. Do not use a slide-deck handout. That is what you are there for!

Be different from everybody else. Stand out and stand up. The originality just might take you somewhere special. At the very least, people will respond and remember what you shared.

CHAPTER 15 NEXT STEPS

☐ Start your "Daily Practice" of writing 10 ideas a day. Ask your staff, "What part of our 'tradition' do we need to reconsider?" Model what you are thinking, and start a dialogue. Read *The Compelling Communicator* and/or "Really Bad PowerPoint," and start presenting in a way that is effective and humane!

CHAPTER SIXTEEN

Class and Achievement

Desegregate Schools

In 1954, the Supreme Court of the USA heard *Brown v. Board of Education*. At the end of this landmark case, the Supreme Court found that laws segregating schools were unconstitutional. This was a profound win for civil rights. Unfortunately, this dream was never fully realized.

Although some schools welcome students from all backgrounds and in some ways celebrate diversity, systematic racism in the form of segregation is still real today, some 50+ years later.

If you do not agree, let me at least share my experience, or you can check out the CNN article by Tami Lubby, "Chicago: America's most segregated city" online. A simple Google search will help you understand the systematic policies that denied poor families of color access to jobs and real estate (and, therefore, good schools).

As an educator in Chicago, I saw firsthand how segregated the schools were. That is because the neighborhoods were segregated as a result of The Chicago Real Estate Board and racially unfair real-estate laws controlling who had access to which homes in the city. By controlling the credit people used to purchase homes, the access people of color had to homes in specific neighborhoods, and the strategic building of public transportation, Chicago was carved up and divided into white and nonwhite neighborhoods. If you are interested in learning more, a quick article "Chicago Isn't Just Segregated, It Basically Invented Modern Segregation" is a good place to start (chicagomag.com/city-life/March-2017/Why-Is-Chicago-So-Segregated).

In Chicago, schools are predominantly "neighborhood" schools. Black kids go to black schools because they live in black neighborhoods. Schools are still segregated. The title of a *US News* May 2016 article put it this way: "More than 60 Years after Brown v. Board of Education School Segregation Still Exists."

As a high school student, I was aware that I went to school with African-American and Latino students, but they were never in my classes. That is because within an integrated school, *the classes were segregated.* They were not segregated in terms of stating this is a "white" class and that one is a "black" class. Instead, they were segregated in a sense by "tracking." Caucasian students typically were enrolled in advanced classes such as AP while students of color were enrolled in "regular" classes.

The major problem with this is twofold for me, although more problems absolutely exist.

Problem #1: Lack of Access to Great Schools

Schools are funded by property taxes and therefore are unequally funded. NPR has a great article explaining this inequity. The idea is simple. In neighborhoods with more businesses and nicer homes, the schools have more funding due to a larger tax base. If neighborhoods are segregated, this means the best (funded) schools are situated in only the most affluent neighborhoods. These schools typically spend more per student and are able to pay staff a much higher salary, therefore attracting the most talented teachers. The poor lose and will never win in this equation. It is mathematically impossible.

Problem #2: Lack of Opportunity to Learn from Each Other

As a leader, I make my worst mistakes when I am unable to think from another's perspective. A segregated school means students are not exposed to different ways of thinking and different lived experiences. That means a white student's experience may never be interrupted or challenged because she never learns what it is like to grow up brown in America. Without this understanding of diversity specifically in the US, it will take that white student much more work to understand complex societal issues that she may never have experienced and vice versa. Her African-American peer will have a hard time understanding her Caucasian peer's experience. One solution could be for schools to host intentional conversations where students tell their stories in order to promote understanding. Another good step would be to investigate Becki Cohn-Vargas's work or the Disruptive Equity Education Project led by Dr. Darnisa Amante.

Without a forum (school) to interact with, discuss, and learn from, how will society truly advance if we limit our ability to be exposed to diversity of thought and experience?

For those who have never had to face complicated realities, it is much easier to believe in the American ethos of "pulling yourself up by your bootstraps" or that poor people should just "work harder."

Fund Schools, not Wars

According to the website Attn, the US spends nearly eight times more on the military than it does on education.

That startling stat should be repeated . . .

The US spends eight times more on the military than it does on education.

In real numbers, that is $598.5 billion vs. $70 billion. I do not remember where I heard this idea, but I subscribe to it. **"Show me how you spend your money and your time, and you will show me your priorities."**

The US spends a lot protecting its political and financial interests through funding a strong military. I would argue that is because we are accustomed to a certain way of life and want to maintain, expand, and protect that ideal.

I am not arguing whether that is a worthy investment or not, nor am I arguing that education should have a budget equal to the military's $598.5 billion.

But what would happen if we added $100 billion more to equally fund schools? What would happen if every school across the US had the same amount to spend, or better yet, those in disadvantaged schools had more to spend to catch up to those who are more privileged?

What would happen if we invested in education and young minds instead of military strength and strong borders?

Would this lead to the collapse of a nation by focusing on education?

Design Matters

Beautiful design matters. Design matters in every aspect of our lives from the homes we choose to the devices that we keep tethered to our hips each day. We choose things not only because of how they look, but how they make us feel.

I am typing this manifesto using a MacBook Pro and the combination of the app Evernote (first draft) and Google Docs (2nd draft).

Why? Design matters.

I like my Mac because of its design. It is simple and clean. It feels sophisticated and even makes me feel more creative as I use it. That is a part of their marketing plan, and it works. And I do not care because I want to feel creative as I compose manifestos, blog posts, and podcasts. Creativity is at the essence of what I do. Years ago, I switched to a Mac because I wanted a tool that was simple and out of the box just worked.

Apple scratched that itch for me, and I have not looked back since. The keyboard layout to the app designs and universal look, to the notification sounds and the way it seamlessly syncs across all devices just works. I like that.

Evernote also just works. It is free or paid-for. I use the paid-for app so that I can have more storage, better security, and an advanced search. Those items are important to me. Evernote also has a clean interface, and with its tagging system, I can organize all 2,609 of my notes and find them within seconds. For example, this book was organized with the tag ".soul" and ".book" . . . it just works.

Google docs also just works. It is incredibly collaborative, it stores and saves within the cloud, and I can add a running Table of Contents as I type, building momentum and excitement for the manifesto!

The condo I stayed in while living in Texas I chose because of design. It is a modern, urban setting within a lively neighborhood of Montrose in Houston, TX. The lobby smells wonderful; the concierge is incredibly friendly; and the valet always talks to me about work, family, and my day (and I reciprocate, of course). The staff and structure of my home make me feel like I matter. Design matters.

So why are schools so archaic? Sure, there are some modern designed schools that I wish I could be a student at, but they are few and far between.

Think about it this way.

Is your school comfortable? Does it promote deep thinking, energy, and active engagement with content and peers? Is your school designed in such a way that kids and adults are excited and proud to be there? If not, why not?

What could happen if we designed schools intentionally so that kids could not wait to go just because they enjoyed—no, loved—being at such a wonderfully designed school?

Living in Trees

I love the fantastical book, *The Baron in the Trees* by the wordsmith Italo Calvino. In this text, a young nobleman, Cosimo, rebels against both his family and noble society at large by deciding to spend the rest of his days in the trees. The story is told from his brother's point of view, narrating Cosimo's escapades high above the ground you and I inhabit.

Throughout the story, Cosimo embarks on a number of adventures, gets into plenty of mischief, and even experiences romance among the trees. He becomes larger than life, and the villagers on the ground tell tall tales that describe his abilities in mythological terms.

Cosimo would have been a fantastic school leader because he had solid principles that governed his life. He was clear on what he stood for, and his mind was made up. These principles guided all his decisions; he never looked back.

I like how Pat Lencioni describes core values. They are the values that not only drive your organization, but you would willingly get punished for living them out.

Freedom, simplicity, and honor were Cosimo's core values. He rejected the opulence of his noble upbringings and declared that he would spend the rest of the days in the trees; his feet would never touch the ground as long as he lived.

As a school leader, what principles do you stand for? Are your convictions real enough to the extent that you would reject comfort, tradition, and acclaim for doing what was right because it aligned with your personal vision?

I don't think we should necessarily start schools over and build them in trees, but what if we did?

The metaphor I think school leaders should tease out is to think deeply about school.

Guided by the strength of our principles, how would we build school if we scrapped the (not so) modern idea of school and rebuilt it from the ground up?

At the end of each podcast, I ask my guest, "You are building a school from the ground up. You are not limited by budget or resources. Your only limitation is your imagination. How would you build your dream school, and what would be your top three priorities?"

I dare you to dream like Cosimo. Reject the modern version of school. Jump into the trees and create a school that amazes and delights its students.

Grades

I love the statement "What gets measured gets done." It illustrates the importance of having a plan and then measuring your progress toward it. Too often, plans are broken from the beginning, and there are many (fixable) issues that with a framework and mindset shift, productivity and impact can exponentially improve. Don't believe me? Join me in one of my productivity webinars, and see for yourself.

Measuring means the something is important, and teams will work toward goals they know "count."

Grades are similar. Most students want to work for the "A." They want the approval that their work matters. Students want to see progress.

But in my opinion, the way we grade students is also broken.

Bonus points for Kleenex . . .

Inordinate percentages used for homework and/or class participation . . .

How we grade also determines how students behave.

Does it matter if a kid never does homework but can still ace your class? What does this say about the meaningless quality of tasks we sometimes ask students to do?

I can see it from both sides.

It is important to teach students the importance of follow through and that sometimes you have to do activities that are uninspiring to you.

But why?

Today's world is evolving fast. The barriers to create the exact job that you want is more accessible these days than it was decades ago.

This brings us to the question, "Why would we ever settle to do uninspiring work?"

In my opinion, grades should reflect mastery of content. Mastery is assessed on formal tests of knowledge: essays, projects, and presentations where students demonstrate a depth of knowledge (not multiple choices tomfoolery).

How much and to what extent students prepare for these demonstrations of understanding should be up to them. No homework? Fine. If you can demonstrate competence and understanding with the amount of practice you need to get there, who am I to judge?

I am willing to give up that power of making students "do stuff." How about you?

This is the ultimate form of personalization. Give students more pathways . . . more voice and choice. Not only on topics they care to learn about, but pathways in which to get there.

If we change the system, we just might be surprised at the amazing results we get. It has been my experience when I have challenged students to show up, they always exceeded expectations.

That is the funny thing about expectations, and John Lubbock said it best:

"What we see depends mainly on what we look for."

Dinosaurs and Building Castles in the Sand

Personalization is a big buzzword right now, a hot topic, and I agree it is a shift we need to make more predominant in schools across the globe. Core subjects and content are important, but how would schools change if we allowed —no, encouraged—students to explore topics of interest to them, consistently?

When I was a kid, I loved learning about dinosaurs. This love affair started in 3rd grade where Mrs. B transferred *her love* of dinosaurs to her students. The year's theme revolved around dinosaurs; we studied them from every angle and every chance we had. The year ended with a trip to the Field Museum in Chicago, where we saw Sue, the infamous skeleton of a gigantic T-Rex that towers above museum-goers in the lobby. She is quite impressive.

I also loved playing outside. We had a sandbox, and as often as I could, I would build sand castles, insert the hose from the back yard, turn the water on, and watch the sand castle explode. I would do this over and over again.

At the University of Illinois at Urbana-Champaign, I worked with preservice teachers in early childhood education. My experience has always been middle and high school so it was quite the opportunity to see how Pre-K and Kindergartens run.

Middle school, high school, and universities should all run more like a kindergarten.

- There is play time or recess consistently . . . awesome!
- The teachers are generally warm and compassionate with students . . .
- There is plenty of show-and-tell . . .
- Students have ample time to learn how to socialize and share . . .
- And most importantly, kids drive the instruction.
- Do you want to learn about oceans? Let's do it!
- Coding? No problem!
- Build an airplane? Absolutely!

We do not have to look far to see how to perfect personalization. It has been occurring in kindergarten for decades.

Want to learn how to be a kindergarten and personalization expert? Check out Jessica Cabeen (@JessicaCabeen). You will be happy you did. She was also my guest on Episode 078 of the podcast.

Start a Seminar Project

I will eat crow on this one. I have to admit that I objected to the idea of seminar when it started at Brooks College Prep, but I was proven wrong. The program thrived and kids benefited along the way.

Each year, our teachers voted on a creative schedule that included seminar. Every nine days of school, we would extend the school day so that every other Wednesday could be a half-day seminar. Students checked into their advisory class (homeroom) and then participated in two 90-minute seminars. These seminars were diverse and included topics like:

- Robotics
- Animation
- Dance (Salsa, Two-Step, etc.)
- Creating music (live and producing in studio)
- Yoga
- Braiding natural hair
- Zumba
- Comics
- And so much more

I always loved the idea of seminar classes. My two objections were:

1. Juniors were forced to take ACT prep, and it was very stressful herding them into those classes. They did not want to be there, and it was painstaking to convince them to go.
2. Some teachers did not take seminar seriously. Thus, the classes they offered sucked and/or they would allow students to roam the halls instead of attend class.

So both objections were more systematic and something we could impact as a leadership team. The key that took seminars from good to great is when Shannae Jackson had the vision for a seminar day. This was a culminating event that occurred at the end of both seminars. On this day, students presented a semester-long project they had been working on in class. Some of these presentations were duds; the best presentations were the live music classes and other performances we had set up in common spaces or even outside. The overall feel around campus was positive and exciting. Seminar Day became another proud tradition found in the culture.

Learning Outside the Walls of the School

The times I was most engaged in learning often occurred outside the walls of school:

- The environment was better (e.g. more creative, relaxing or stimulating, etc.).
- I was working on something I wanted to learn about (personalization).
- There was often a mentor/hands-on component (authentic).

Making learning relevant should be an integral part of each school. We should be engaged in more questioning and listening to find out exactly what it is students have questions about and want to learn. If we did that, I wonder how student engagement would be impacted?

The modern student does not even watch TV anymore.

Entertainment disruptors like Netflix and YouTube have created an a-la-carte and individualized programming option for students to watch.

Heck . . . I do not even watch TV anymore.

Celebrities are found on social media. Live feeds and "stories" from FB, Instagram, and Snapchat are where our students turn for entertainment. It is all happening on smartphones.

In a class of 30 students, they very well can be "tuned in" to 30 different programs. What are we doing as schools that makes learning integrated with tech, on demand, and highly personalized?

If we do not change, how will student engagement be impacted?

Celebrate Kids Every Step of the Way

"Children should be seen and not heard" is one of the stupidest proverbs I have ever read. Too often school is designed to make things comfortable for the adults, not the kids.

Think about it . . . what kid likes to

- stand in line?
- remain sitting, quiet at their desk for 45 minutes?

- work independently instead of in a group?
- sit through an entire lunch period (at their table) without getting up?
- wear an ID badge or uniform?
- do homework?
- hang out with peers only their age?

In fact, what adult likes to do those things, either? I asked on Instagram, "Are schools designed for adults or for students?" A bunch of people weighed in. I would love to read your opinion, too. Check out the post in my resource download of the book and leave a comment. So instead of making schools so adult-centric, how can we focus on kids and make it a better experience for them? Isn't it ironic that we are even discussing this question? The whole point of schools is to serve kids!

A lot of the ideas above are about control and creating (or forcing through an abuse of power) an "orderly" environment . . . one that benefits the adults.

I love this Zig Ziglar quote: **"You can have everything in life that you want, if you will just help enough other people get what they want."**

Replace "enough other people" with "your students" in the above quote, and it still rings true. I wonder what would happen in schools if we considered this quote every day, serving kids first, and helping them get what they want . . . every . . . single . . . day.

"You can have everything in life that you want, if you will just help your students get what they want."

I will bet my lunch money that test scores would go up (or whatever other metric you care about). More importantly, I bet kids would feel a lot more connected and engaged in the school.

Part of being a successful podcast host is helping the listeners see the guest as a "hero." I learned that in the Spring of 2016, listening to an interview with Don Miller on *Entreleadership* while working on the schedules of 900 high school students.

We Need to Make Our Students the Heroes of the School Every Day

Google PBIS and look how you can incorporate a systematic way to celebrate student success . . . every . . . single . . . day.

Help kids get what they want, celebrate them and make them feel like a hero (every single one of them), and I guarantee you will create a powerful school, and I do not mean celebrating mediocrity. That is stupid. No one gets a medal for coming in 4th place. The challenge is to look for the gold in side of every single student. It is there. It is your job to find it. If you cannot, that is a deeper issue inside of you.

Celebrate Adults Every Day, Too.

Just like celebrating kids, celebrating staff members is super-duper important. A year or two ago, I crowdsourced a popular post on my blog, "Staff Appreciation Ideas." In this post, 12 school leaders share their ideas on how best to celebrate their staff members. The Photo Booth idea from Suzanne Mitchell is a real winner. In fact, Suzanne is probably the best leader I know at coming up with creative ways to celebrate staff. In order to take this to a whole new level, she developed a team she calls her "Directors of WOW." She was my guest on Episode 074 and drops major value around staff celebration on the episode.

My favorite way to celebrate stay members was to organically allow the community to nominate staff and then vote on the winners. I delegated the running of the team to an awesome AP at my school (shout out to Hillary . . . you are freaking amazing!). Each month, students, staff, and parents would nominate staff members.

KEY POINT: everyone's name was on the list from the admin and teachers to the cafe workers and custodians. Everyone matters!

First, through a simple Google Form, people chose a staff member. Next, the nominator chose a value the nominee exemplified (e.g. going the extra mile). Then, the nominator wrote how the staff member lived out this value on a day-to-day basis. Lastly, the nominator had the opportunity to add any other important information they wanted to share about what made the nominee an amazing person. The nominations went to our team members, who voted each month on a winner. Every single nominee received a paper that shared exactly what was written about them, and the winner was announced at our regular morning staff meeting. Just like the students, the staff needs to be celebrated and should be the heroes of the building.

Create this kind of climate, and people will be knocking down your door to serve the students of your community. And if all else fails . . . do what Jimmy Casas does at the beginning of every What Great Educators Do Differently Conference. Play some lively music and tell everyone to dance, hug, and high-five each other all while finding five people to look in the eye and say, "You are awesome!" That will always fill a room with smiles and laughter!

Tech Tools Do Not Equal Deep Learning

I am in love with technology. Many readers have this book in their hands today because they found me through my website, podcast, or maybe an online bookstore. Maybe that is true of you, maybe not.

There are many incredible tech tools that educators engage in to innovate and connect with their students in a modern way. I applaud these efforts. Yet, I am skeptical to the broader use of technology, and I wonder if it masks surface-level thinking.

A pig with lipstick is still a pig.

Just because you are using the latest technology does not mean students are engaged in meaningful, relevant, and authentic learning.

I can leverage the power found in my iPhone and type the words that you are reading here right now, or I can spend the next three hours playing Candy Crush without contributing anything meaningful to society.

Of course there is a time and place for leisure, but in the context of school, I am urging educators to use technology intentionally.

Does it advance the broader unit goal or allow the student to engage with the content in a new or deeper way?

A worksheet on an iPad is still a worksheet and does not constitute the one-on-one tech Silicon Valley would appreciate.

Depth over devices. Devices are just a supplement to the core of the curriculum.

Tell the School's Story on Social Media

Many school leaders fear social media, but they should not. I am guessing that you do not if you are reading this book. We probably crossed paths on social media at some point: Twitter, FB, Insta, or maybe you found me via my website or podcast.

School leaders wear many different hats. We also lack a budget to hire people to fulfill all the roles expected of us. So congratulations, you are now the marketing director for your school, too.

That is not a bad thing, and with just a little effort, you can do a very good job.

It now literally pays to tell your story on social media. There are plenty of companies and individuals looking for a good cause to support. Your school should be that cause. By sharing compelling articles, images, and micro-stories through social media, you can get noticed. The key to building a platform is consistency and value.

Even if you have all the funds you need, both parents and students will appreciate you telling your school's story via social media.

Just Google kids and TV, and you will see that since 2015, numerous reports have been shared on the internet that kids watch internet video such as YouTube more than they do TV.

If you want to influence kids (and more and more adults), their eyeballs are on their mobile device. Savvy school leaders will leverage technology to get noticed by their community. Sharing important school-related and inspiring information via social media is almost a necessity, and it is a great way to build relationships with students and families outside of school.

There are barely any barriers to building a platform for your school. You do not need a marketing agency. You do not have to write a press release and pray your story gets picked up. In most cases, you just create a log-on and start telling your story. If you create a podcast, you only have to invest in some nominal fees to distribute the show and buy some startup gear. These are my favorite places to share stories:

- Twitter
- Instagram (including Insta stories)
- FB, FB Groups (your school should have one), and FB Live
- Snapchat (Yes!)
- LinkedIn
- Podcasts

New Ways to Interview

I think we need a new way to interview in education. The traditional way of identifying "A" players for your organization are out of date and ineffective. Most schools rely on a standard set of questions that probably are the same from school to school generally speaking.

These probably include:

1. Tell me about yourself.
2. What is your greatest strength/weakness?
3. Why do you want to work here?
4. What is your philosophy of education?
5. How would you teach _____?
6. How would you respond to _____ situation?

Snooze. BORING!

Wake me up when something relevant and meaningful is asked. I suggest aligning our interview to the mission, vision, and values of the organization.

Do you even have a real mission, vision, and core values for your school? Are they real? Do they guide what you do in your organization day to day? If you need help developing mission, vision, and values within your organization, I can help.

Sunshine High School values *Going Above and Beyond.* I think they would like to hire folks that actually live this out.

> **Beginner:** Ask during the interview for a story when they went above and beyond in their work and over-delivered.

> **Black Belt:** When the candidate arrives for the interview coach your main office staff to manufacture some type of project and/or emergency they need help with (e.g. making copies and delivering to teachers). Ask the candidate to help. Main office staff takes notes on the candidate's response.

> **Jedi:** Choose a real problem that the school faces. During the initial interview, ask them to design a solution to present at a follow-up interview (only do this with candidates you are serious about hiring).

Or another example: **Macaroni Middle School values *Collaboration.***

> **Beginner:** Ask for examples of stories where they were a part of a collaborative team. Dig deep. Ask why the team was successful or struggled. Note how they answer. Do they talk more about themselves, or do they talk about how they played a role and how others also contributed to the team? Pay attention to the tone of the conversation.

> **Black Belt:** Ask a number of candidates to work on designing an RtI cycle together. Have them analyze data. Design an assessment and follow up intervention/acceleration activities. Then the candidates present this cycle to the interview team. Not only can you evaluate the quality of

the work of the candidates, you can also observe their ability to work together. You can even participate in the group and see who you like working with!

Jedi: Have candidates do some type of group activity together (e.g. human pretzel). Have everyone stand in a circle and interlock their arms and hands. Then see how they unwind themselves from this human knot. Leadership and collaborative skills are easily observable during this fun (and sometimes tense) activity. Or why not have candidates play some type of board game or physical game (basketball) against each other? It does not matter the game; the point is to see how people work together.

A Few More Ideas

I hear from so many industries outside of education where candidates and hiring officials meet outside the organization. In New York, it is quite common to go for a walk with someone hiring for a financial position on Wall Street.

In his book, *Never Eat Alone,* Keith Ferrazzi shares that he interviews while playing racquetball (a sport he loves) or going for a light jog.

Why does this matter? An interview in a tired conference room is a stale and artificial environment where you can get to know someone. Get outside and do something fun. I guarantee you are going to get to know the person better.

If your community values service and selflessness, volunteer somewhere together. If a person flinches, great! They were not the right fit anyway.

How about inviting a candidate (and her partner) to dinner with you and your partner? How a candidate carries herself at dinner and how she interacts with your partner will tell you a lot about her (and how she will interact with staff and students). If you can enjoy a meal together, you probably can enjoy working together.

Of course, you cannot do this for every teacher candidate, but with positions carrying more influence (e.g. department chairs, instructional coaches, APs), I think we can put in more effort and more creativity.

Your school deserves it.

CHAPTER 16 NEXT STEPS

- ☐ Be a champion of diversity. Celebrate all cultures represented in the nation, and fight to desegregate schools.

- ☐ Reflect on ways you can change the design of your school to make it more engaging for kids and a better work environment for adults.

- ☐ Identify your core principles or values. Evaluate your decisions through this lens.

- ☐ Start a seminar day at your school. Rethink your interview process. You can do better. Make sure you are testing to see your core values displayed in an applicant. You can teach people how to teach, but you cannot make them better people or the right fit for your organization.

CHAPTER SEVENTEEN

Staff and Students Working Together

Paulo Freire

I was introduced to Paulo Freire in college and read his seminal text, *Pedagogy of the Oppressed*. This book framed my career trajectory in education and molded my educational mindset.

Two main ideas hit me like a lightning bolt that I want to share with you.

POWERFUL AND HUMANIZING EDUCATION

In the text, Freire unpacks the relationship between the oppressor and oppressed. Another way to think of it is the haves and have-nots. In the US, we have the saying to describe people "from the wrong side of the tracks." Those are the oppressed. Normally they represent people of color and those that live in poverty. Education is the key to liberation.

This happens when the oppressed take ownership of their learning. The oppressed iterate the core content and take it from its roots emulating the lives of the oppressor and make it their own. This kind of education also challenges the oppressor to investigate his own existence and how he contributes to the oppression of his neighbors.

TEACHERS AND THE BANKING MODEL

Traditionally, some teachers (and I as a naive undergrad) thought of teachers as being of higher worth. I was the teacher, and in that role, I had much knowledge to bestow on my students . . . how lucky for them! Many educators think of themselves in equally haughty terms.

We view our students as empty containers that must be filled with our superior knowledge and experience. This actually takes ownership and liberation away from our students and places them in the role of the oppressed. They are passive. They receive knowledge from us . . . the expert teacher. It is a controlling perspective of education. The antidote is an environment that promotes curiosity, risk-taking, learning from failure, and one that celebrates the diversity, expertise, and experiences the students bring into the classroom. The approach Freire suggests is one that asks students to take a leadership role through solving interesting problems they face in life. It is much like personalized learning and authentic project/problem-based learning.

Paulo Coelho

Mr. Coehlo is the author of one of my favorites of all time books, *The Alchemist*. I first read this in college for a class that prepared me to be an English teacher. I read it a second time after I met the love of my life, Miriam. At the time, we were exploring her opportunity to create a global health program in Antwerp, Belgium. It was a tough decision to make, one that involved great risk but also great reward. I remembered how *The Alchemist* moved me in a profound way, and I wanted to share that experience with her. The protagonist in the book is a shepherd who finds his personal legend to fulfill. We decided that fate, the cosmos, maybe even God, had put Antwerp in our path, and we said yes to the job and the adventure that awaits us in Belgium.

I believe everyone has a personal legend to fulfill. We all have greatness inside us and a story that we must personally embark on filled with challenges and triumphs. It is our destiny to find the narrative of that story and follow its path to the end. What do you think your personal legend might be? I would love to know!

Who knew if you are named Paulo and are Brazilian you would have profoundly impacted my thinking? Maybe I should consider naming a future son Paulo. I have always loved the name!

Honey Empires

If I visited your school or organization and had the opportunity to interview anyone, how would they respond to the following question? How does (INSERT YOUR NAME) treat you? How does (INSERT YOUR NAME) make you feel at work? What words and actions contribute to this feeling? In the section labeled, "Clouds and Dirt," I cited some ideas that I learned from Gary Vee. Here he has impacted my leadership yet again.

In his videos, Gary loves to talk about creating a "honey empire."

According to Gary, **"The honey part means I am going to change the world . . . the empire part means I will do it at all costs."**

I have also noted that Gary talks quite a bit about self-awareness and empathy. These components are also integral to a Honey Empire.

Self-awareness allows the leader to consider and reflect on his ego, motives, how he treats others, and how he is perceived. Insight is crucial because it allows the leader to exist outside of a bubble and truly make decisions that are thoughtful of others' experiences within the organization. Empathy is foundational to a successful Honey Empire. Without it, we cannot connect with another's experience in our organization and will be destined to make decisions that are misaligned with what both the organization and its people need.

Schools are uniquely positioned to be long-standing Honey Empires.

Education is compulsory in most nations and helps provide society with contributing members that can critically think on their own.

What other type of organization has such an opportunity? Every day, we are blessed with the opportunity to make a difference in the lives of the students and communities we serve.

We can change the world.

We can create lasting change. The lasting change is our empire's story. The honey is based off the way we handle our staff and students with compassion while acting on an inspiring vision that will change the world.

Dirt to Diamonds

In 2016, 1,500 11–13-year-old students walked onto my campus to engage in the day's lessons and socialize with their peers. At that age, the students are filled with so much possibility and wonder. Really at any age, a student sits in front of her teacher like raw material that can be shaped into something beautiful. Although students are not empty vessels into which we pour our knowledge, they are under our care to mold and model into champions of the human race.

Through creating a healthy, welcoming, connected, and curious environment, the teacher chisels away at the student and forms something new. I see teaching and leadership a lot like Michelangelo saw sculpting:

"Every block of stone has a statue inside it, and it is the task of the sculptor to discover it."

Do you take that approach in teaching and leadership? Do you see the humans you interact with every day as raw material with something magical inside?

That is the beauty of the teacher–student relationship. It is actually a reciprocal relationship. It is active. The teacher changes the student as much as the student influences a metamorphosis in the teacher. Both influence each other tremendously.

This happens through dialogue and genuine curiosity. When groups of people collaborate to solve interesting problems, something beautiful happens as a result.

What first just seemed raw material . . . maybe even dirt . . . is slowly refined throughout the course of an expertly planned unit.

And that dirt slowly is formed into a diamond.

The sculpture is formed.

When I taught Senior English, I taught a Critical Theory class. We looked at a number of different ideas from Feminism to Deconstructionism.

My class, situated on the Far South Side of Chicago, was introduced to these ideas for the very first time. Our feminist unit specifically was incredibly rewarding. Simply by exploring advertisements from the '50s until modern times and applying a feminist lens, students were able to investigate how women are portrayed and (mis)represented by companies looking to make a buck or two.

Are the advertisements right or wrong? Judging was not the point. Offering another tool with which students could experience the world with was the point. Now they had a tool to think deeply about what was shown to them constantly each day and how it influences their thinking. Dirt formed into diamonds, and students intellectually evolved just a bit more.

Do Not Feed the Sharks

When there is blood in the water, the sharks come to feed . . .

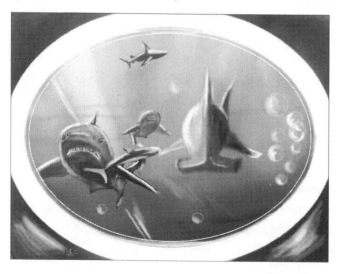

It never made a lot of sense to me, but disciplining children when an adult is angry is never a good idea. We all need to breathe and take a step back from the situation. I found it uncomfortable when a teacher came into my office hot and heavy with a kid in tow . . . maybe even screaming about the child's offenses and how I need to discipline the child who "gets away with everything." I think the idea of grace would be helpful here as well as a 15-minute time-out. On the topic of the time-out, my wife Miriam shared an interesting idea I had never really considered before. Time-outs are more for the adult than they are the child. The time-out allows for the adult to regain control and logic over their reptilian minds, which allows them to mete out discipline and correction with compassion, patience, and empathy for the child.

Do not get me wrong . . . kids need to face consequences for their actions. I have the opinion that the best teacher is not in the form of detached punishment that does not teach the child a powerful life lesson. That is why detention and suspension do not work. What do they really teach?

I am a believer in restorative practices. There are a million resources on the web about this approach to discipline. I linked two restorative practices resources in the companion resource to this book available on my website.

I love restorative practices for a few reasons. Kids (and adults) learn that in every negative interaction some type of "harm" or "damage" occurs in a relationship, and this harm can be repaired. The repairing of a relationship puts ownership in the hands of the individual who caused the harm. This ownership is often a powerful teacher. Life lessons are learned (and rarely repeated) because of this power. More ownership is also transferred to students when running a Peer Council that hears cases and deliberates on effective ways for an individual to repair a relationship. I found it much more powerful to have a peer sit in front of his or her peers and share what he or she did and receive a consequence, than it is receiving one from a dean.

And a final problem with traditional discipline is that it uses fear, power, and intimidation to motivate. That is wrong. What are we teaching our children through the traditional discipline model in most schools? What are we teaching kids about making wrong choices, learning from mistakes, and ultimately redemption?

We cannot talk out both sides of our mouth. We cannot claim to value making and learning from our mistakes while punishing each misstep along the way. I recently interviewed Mike Acomb, a principal outside of Cleveland. One of his school's values is the courage to learn from our mistakes. When kids learn from their mistakes, a system response is triggered. The kid is celebrated by the teacher, who gives the student a sticker. This celebrates that the student learned from a mistake and the sticker recognizes this too. Then the student is sent to the principal's office—not for punishment, but to share the powerful story of learning. Mike takes a picture of the student and displays it in the hall for all to see. Mike then wraps up this exchange by calling or texting the parent to communicate how proud he is that the student learned from their mistake. I imagine that this conversation continues at the dinner table and from what I understand, Mike's older students are now celebrating this value in the younger ones, perpetuating this wonderful cultural value.

My Student Is the Hero

The hero's journey . . . If you understand this narrative structure, you can create an interesting story. Here is a simple breakdown of the hero's journey:

- There is a hero who embarks on an adventure.
- The hero faces a crisis and emerges victorious.
- The hero returns home changed or transformed.

I heard a podcast once frame the job of the podcaster as making the guest a hero when she stars on the show. In terms of business, the client must be seen as a hero. With these ideas in mind, why not use the hero's journey in school leadership? Can't the student, staff member, parent, or community member be the hero each day in schools across the globe? This concept matters for school leadership.

If you are like me, there may be a default setting in your human programming that says, "I want to be the hero . . . I want the acclaim, the awards, the recognition . . ." I admit, that is probably a natural way to feel, especially as the leader. You are the one putting in blood, sweat, tears, and countless hours into accomplishing the vision of the school. But we must avoid this natural disposition and subdue our egos. If we can frame the challenges we face and celebrate the successes of our organization while promoting our people as the heroes and not taking the credit ourselves, we are better suited to take our organizations even further. If we establish everyone else as heroes in the narrative of our day-to-day school work, people will feel seen, heard, and celebrated. As a teacher, if my boss told me I was a hero and that my work mattered, what wouldn't I do for him? Finally, thinking about the hero's journey in terms of narrative structure, answer the following questions:

1. How am I crafting experiences that can be seen as adventures for my school community?
2. How am I helping my community experience success when facing challenges?
3. How am I celebrating the wins in my community and illustrating the transformation that is happening in our school?

As a leader, it is your job to make everyone else a hero. Do this and you will be a hero.

Shadow a Kid

Progressing through the leadership ranks can distance you from the classroom and the student experience if you are not careful. As the years go by, a leader can become more and more out of touch with the reality of what happens day to day in school. Soon you exist in a bubble, unable to relate to what happens in education.

School leaders stay connected through observations, eating lunch in the cafeteria with kids, even teaching a class or two. Another great way to stay connected with the student experience is to participate in a shadow day. I was speaking with someone off the record who has been on the podcast and is a popular guest. He holds a high-level position at the district level. It was shocking to hear what his shadow experience was like. This was not an unannounced shadow visit. On some level, he worried that the "dog and pony" show would be in full effect. Nope. Which was good. He was able to see how the student he shadowed experienced the school day. The shocking results . . . four scheduled major assessments in one day (out of an eight-period schedule . . . one being lunch). He was exhausted (and incredibly bored) watching the painful experience this student went through. Didn't the teachers communicate with each other regarding when they might give a major assessment? Where was the empathy for what was expected of the students? For better or worse, you can get an inside look at what is and is not happening within your school or district by simply shadowing a kid.

Meet with Students Regularly

In addition to shadowing students to get an insider's look at the school experience, school leaders must meet with kids regularly. Of course you can learn a lot about the school experience, but more importantly, it will give you an opportunity to give back and grow your students through intentional mentorship.

I suggest selecting through an application process a subset of each grade level to make up a student–principal advisory board. They can speak into school-related issues, but through this vehicle, you can mentor these young leaders via managing their projects. There is a lot to learn through starting an initiative and seeing it through completion. Even if the project fails, lessons are learned.

If you do decide to set up a principal's advisory board and run it through applications, think about how you might get at the unheard and invisible voices within your school. Consider saving a few "seats" to handpick students that might not typically show the initiative or consider joining such an experience. This might be the shot they do not even know they are looking for, and you can alter someone's path in life by giving them a chance.

These meetings can take place before or after school, or if you have a special schedule, within the school day. I met with my group during a "seminar" class period that met every other Wednesday morning within the school day.

Leaders reproduce themselves and give back. Are you mentoring your students?

Solving Problems

Death by worksheets is an all-too-common malady that faces modern students. It is easy for the teacher and helps control classes of kids, but we didn't get into teaching for the power and control aspect, did we?

At home, I was asked to solve problems to get what I wanted.

That new comic book. How would I afford *that* without any money?

I had to come up with a solution . . . enter my first job at the comic shop, Fat Dutchies in Palatine, IL. I convinced the owner, Chuck, to hire me. I counted inventory of comics so he knew how many to order in the future. My payment was pizza or Italian beef, some comics, and $20.

This is just one example of the millions of problems I had to solve while at home.

How will you afford that comic?

When a student faces a problem or policy they want to change at school, what is the common administrative response?

No . . .

That is not in our student handbook (policy) . . .

(Other weak excuse) . . .

Why is students' creativity for solving problems shut down so quickly? Order? Control?

Meanwhile, the worksheets fly off the copiers and into the teacher's hand.

Children are forced to solve interesting problems at home. Why not at school?

Two ways to solve this problem are with project-based learning and design thinking.

I have interviewed two experts on project-based learning: John Mergondoller from the Buck Institute and Kyle Wagner from Transform Educational Consulting. I also interviewed a teacher-leader who used design thinking to help her students solve a crappy situation at her school here.

Here is my simplistic explanation of project based learning and design thinking into seven steps:

1. Ask your students about problems they see and would like to solve.
2. Research and collect data through surveys, interviews, and observations.
3. Consider the data and identify any trends.
4. Prototype solutions.
5. Administer real solutions.
6. Collect more data.
7. Review your findings. If satisfied with the result, address a new problem. If unsatisfied, iterate.

Ask a Parent How to Improve

The easiest way to improve a school is to ask. It might sound a little scary, and engaging with parents can at times be quite annoying, but if you ask them how to improve the school, you are almost guaranteed to get an answer. Surveys work great for this, but focus groups are even better.

Pick a random slice of all the parents that represent your student population and ask them, "How can we improve the school?" Listen intently, jot down notes, form a committee, and take action. If you respond in this type of way, then you are guaranteed to not only have a better school but to also have garnered more parental support. I find it to be very helpful to get outside the walls of school where group think or the disease of "tradition" can thwart a fledgling new idea that can be a game changer for your community.

Ask, act, and repeat to exist within a continuous cycle of improvement. If you earn the parents' trust through this process, there is no telling to what you can accomplish. A lot of momentum can be built by asking parents what dreams they have for their students and what kind of school they desire to serve their children. Include teachers in this process, and discuss the results consistently. This may just be the spark your community was looking for.

Invite Parents in to Learn

Too often I have observed schools that hold an "Us vs. Them" philosophy with parents. **We are not at war. We are on the same team.** In my opinion, schools should look for as many opportunities as possible to collaborate and invite parents into the school. Not for a cheesy presentation or for the same old Open House, but for some type of authentic experience. Schools keep parents out based on two fears.

- They might see something they do not like (e.g. poor teaching or poor student behavior).
- They might act crazy.

In response, schools can address both issues quite easily. Blemishes should not be covered up. If you make a mistake, that is an opportunity for growth! We all win! And if a parent wants to act crazy? Have a protocol for that. We do not (or should not) tolerate crazy kids or teachers . . . so why tolerate crazy parents?

By multiplying the amount of caring adults in and across a school, the students win.

What if we invited parents in to learn, too? Maybe they would be inspired or with their newfound knowledge be able to tutor kids after school?

What if parents who were experts in systems, service, and operations were able to evaluate how the building functions and then were able to provide and "own" part of the solutions? Again, we all win!

CHAPTER 17 NEXT STEPS

☐ How could you add more "honey" to your organization? Share this Michelangelo quote with your staff: "Every block of stone has a statue inside it and it is the task of the sculptor to discover it."

☐ Have a courageous conversation discussing this topic with your staff.

☐ Consider restorative practices as an alternative to traditional discipline. Are your students, staff, and parents considered "heroes" in your community? What would you need to change to make that a reality?

☐ Shadow a kid for a day or two. Communicate what your experience was like. Consider if any changes need to be made.

☐ Form a Principal Advisory Board made solely of students. Pour into them, challenge them, and make real change based on their ideas.

CHAPTER EIGHTEEN

Building Your School

My Most Popular Question

At the end of every show, I love to ask guests this question: You are building a school from the ground up ... you are not limited by budget or any resources, your only limitation is your imagination ... how would you build your dream school and what would your top three priorities be? For a stretch of episodes, I actually took this question out of the podcast. The listeners revolted ... so I added it back in because what I have learned is that this is the most popular question I ask. I think it is a popular question because it removes all the barriers we currently face in education and asks my guest to dream. The insights shared answering this question can sometimes be massaged and adapted to the current reality of schools. The answers make school a better place. Tony Robbins famously stated ... **"If you want better answers, ask better questions."**

I see that demonstrated at the end of each show. Whether it is on *iTunes* or BetterLeadersBetterSchools.com, you can listen to every episode and every answer from my guests. Here are some themes that I have heard loud and clear:

The Importance of People

Jim Collins used the metaphor of "getting the right people on the bus." We all know it, claim it, and understand the value of great employees that fit our culture. I am not so sure that we will not hire the wrong person or better yet wait to hire the best person. From my experience leading, the wrong people will absolutely destroy your culture. I have seen it firsthand within the faculty and even in my (adopted) leadership team.

The Importance of Space

Earlier, I noted how school design has not really changed since the industrial era. Schools should be like the Magic Kingdom and inspire wonder and creativity. They should be comfortable spaces that kids cannot wait to occupy. Many guests answer with the idea of flexible space and have even commented, "Do we really need a building?" When they say that, guests always recommend taking students out into the world, exploring authentic learning experiences.

The Importance of Curriculum

This answer is not rooted in standards or classics. The idea is grounded in authentic problems that need to be solved within the students' community. You can teach any concept through a vehicle that is important to a student. All we need to do is ask. I would like to see schools incorporate more design thinking and problem-based learning.

The Importance of Compensation

The longest-standing joke in education is that I did not choose this career because of the money. Sadly, it is true, and government abuses the fact that people choose this profession because of passion and impact over financial reward. Ultimately, this leads to some of the best and brightest educators leaving the profession to pursue professions that are less bureaucratic and offer more compensation. I am not arguing that educators need to be compensated the highest in society. In fact, salaries only motivate so much. The idea I present is to pay a fair wage that exceeds inflation and removes any concern about affording a modest lifestyle. If educators are working more than one job to pay the bills, that is a problem. I did it as a young educator, and many young educators I know have a side job during the school year and summer, too.

Savannah Bananas

I wanted to end this book with a story that I hope will challenge your thinking. When I embarked on this journey of writing a book, I generated a list of topics that investigated and explored two ideas:

- What is school for?

- What does it take to be a school leader?

Thank you, Seth Godin, for inspiring me to write this. I want to end the book with the story of Jesse Cole and the Savannah Bananas.

The Savannah Bananas are a "baseball team" that plays in the Coastal Plain League. I put "baseball team" in quotes because before Jesse, the Bananas were just another college summer league baseball team that nobody cared about (or went to their games). That is . . . until Jesse had an epiphany when he took over the team.

He boldly declared to all in the Banana organization: **"We are not a baseball organization . . . we are an entertainment organization."** Everything changed. In *Savannah Now*, you can read "Savannah Bananas Owners Introduce Baseball Appeal at Grayson Stadium." Of course I linked it for you in this book's resource download. Or go to the Bananas website and check out their "About Us" page. I love the picture at the top of this page. There are a bunch of employees in shorts and T-shirts and one crazy guy in a yellow tux (yup . . . that is Jesse). Does this look like your typical baseball front office? When Jesse boldly stated, "We are not a baseball organization . . . we are an entertainment organization," everything changed for the Bananas. It took some time, but now the Bananas have been completely sold out for each game for the past two years (completely unheard of for a college league team).There are two main reasons for this:

- They know exactly who they are.
- They know exactly whom they serve.

Jesse Cole's rallying cry for his organization is "Fans First." You see this in the outrageous entertainment they offer between innings—their players dance in between innings or there are frequent grandma beauty pageants . . . If the game gets rained out, staff will walk you to your car with an umbrella.

When I met Jesse at a conference, he told a story of an intern who went missing for a few hours when a game was cancelled because of rain. She eventually returned to the stadium, and Jesse asked where she had been. Her reply: "I walked an elderly man home. He did not drive to the park. Fans First, right, Jesse?"

This story is a powerful example of how values can lead an organization to greatness. It also illustrates the value of understanding who you are and whom you serve. The Savannah Bananas became a great organization when they realized they were not about baseball but about entertainment.

I wonder what would happen to our underperforming and uninspiring schools if they had a similar epiphany? Schools are not about education. They are about _____. Through this book, I attempted to look at that question and answer it from a number of different angles. I intentionally kept the sentence blank so that you can answer this question for yourself and maybe even write your own manifesto.

What is school for?

Your Manifesto

Thank you for reading this book. *Feel free to share a copy with your friends and colleagues.* Criticize it, or create your own and send me a copy when you are finished! I would be happy to feature it on my blog, email to my list, and maybe have you as a guest on the podcast. Think long and hard about the question, "What is school for?" I would love to see how you would answer that question.

YOU ARE INVITED TO JOIN THE MASTERMIND.

"It takes a village to raise a child." I love this quote because it highlights the importance of community and connection when raising children. The moral: we cannot do it on our own. We cannot do it independently. Yet, we do. Of course some schools are doing a great job with connection, especially through the use of Professional Learning Communities and team teaching models. Some schools have incredibly healthy departments, functioning with an "all hands on deck" ethos serving their community at a high level. The reality is, many teachers and nearly all admin are working in isolation. Of course, you can connect on Twitter, FB, and Voxer. I encourage you to do so! I also welcome you to join the mastermind.

The mastermind is a hybrid group coaching and leadership development community. A year ago, I intentionally decided to keep it small (no more than 60 leaders) so that we could focus on building a group with great depth, intimacy, and trust. If I had a superpower, it would be that of being a great connector. The idea behind the mastermind is quite simple. Each week, I throw a great "party" and invite some of the best leaders in education that I have met.

Because of their commitment to growth and to the mastermind, we are able to achieve a level of depth that your average PLN on Twitter or Voxer just cannot touch because of the sheer size or the lack of commitment to a weekly discussion. Consistently, mastermind members have told me that participating in this group has been the "Best PD I have ever received" and that they joined "to become a better leader, but became a better spouse, parent, and friend instead."

You are invited. Will you join us in the mastermind? If you would like more info, please email me (daniel@betterleadersbetterschools.com) and I will get you the right info and we can set up a call to discuss your future in the group. If this group is too much of a commitment for you at this time, then I welcome you to connect on Twitter (@alienearbud) or email.

WHAT GOES IN MUST COME OUT.

What you consume is very powerful whether it is media, literature, or even the people you hang out with. Have you grown soft or fat? Has your body atrophied? Reflecting on your last week, how much time did you spend in the gym? What kind of resources did you consume? As I have embarked on my own fitness journey, I have come to realize that maybe 10–20% of my body is the effort I put into the gym. The remainder is the foods I choose to consume. That is what led me to cut out pop (or soda if you are not from the Midwest) and even fruit juices because of the extra sugar. I am mostly a water/coffee/tea drinker these days with a glass of wine with dinner and maybe a little more over the weekend. I also drink sparkling water because I like the fizz!

Mentally, we are the same. Media and literature influences how we think, but even more powerful influences are the people we hang out with. I have read many times this idea: **Want to know who you are becoming? Show me the people you hang out with.** If you find yourself irritable, impatient, ineffective, then look at your friends, acquaintances, and (even) your family. The people you choose to hang out with influences you at a high level.

What goes in (the mind and body) must come out. If you want to have a more positive experience and successful life, reflect on the people you hang out with and decide if they are good and healthy for you. It is a hard question but one that must be answered to experience all that life has to offer you. The world is an oyster, but if your friends overeat, there may be no oyster left for you.

CHAPTER 18 NEXT STEPS

☐ How would you answer my famous podcast question, "You are building a school from the ground up . . . you are not limited by budget or any resources, your only limitation is your imagination . . . how would you build your dream school and what would your top three priorities be?" How would your staff and parents answer this question?

☐ Study Jesse Cole. Be different and stand out. If his organization wasn't about baseball but entertainment, how does that impact how we view our schools?

☐ Fill in the blank, "Schools are not about education, they are about _____." You might think this statement is crazy, and I assure you, it is. However, Jesse and the Bananas continue to sell out entire seasons to a team nobody cared about just a few years ago. What kind of excitement would this bring to your school community if you courageously answered this question?

☐ Write your own manifesto. If you turn it into a book, email me, and I will check it out. If you do it in the form a blog post or PDF, share it with me, and I will promote it.

☐ Now do this, "When you realize how perfect everything is, you will tilt your head back and laugh at the sky." —Buddha. Go ahead, tilt your head back, and have a good laugh for me. You deserve it. Life is good.

THANKS

IF YOU ENJOYED THE BOOK but want to get the audio version, you can do so on my website. As a podcaster, I had a lot of fun recording this book, and I added extra content and improvised some chapters, so there is value getting this audio companion in addition to this written one. A few thanks are in order . . .

Thank you to the reader who engaged in this book.

Thank you, Miriam, the love of my life. Your encouraging words, hugs, and kisses kept me going while writing this book. If God asked me to create my ideal mate, I would make her just like you; I would not change one thing.

Thank you to Big A, my mentor. You shared *The 12 Week Year* in our mastermind, which gave me a system to write this book. I wrote on two topics a day, every day for nearly 12 weeks and completed the first draft. The second draft was completed in three weeks. The third draft I completed in one week.

Thank you, Seth Godin for writing *Stop Stealing Dreams,* which inspired me to write my first book for school leaders.

Thanks, Brian Moran, for writing *The 12 Week Year*. Some of your ideas make up the foundation of my goal crushers productivity course.

Thank you, Jaime Jay, for creating the first spreadsheet that I edited to turn into my #GoalCrusher template and Scott Beebe and Jonathan Bates, who taught me how to become a Jedi using systems and processes.

A *big* shout out to my 4 p.m. ISI Mastermind. You guys pushed, challenged, and encouraged me to write this book.

Thank you, Jennifer Abrams, for giving me confidence to "Swim in the deep end" and pursue my dream of serving school leaders full time.

Thank you, Jennifer Harshman. This book would have launched in a big fat mess if I did not have your editing wizardry to clean it up and organize the ideas in a way that makes sense.

Thanks, James Woosley, for designing an attractive book that people can enjoy.

ABOUT THE AUTHOR

DANIEL BAUER (a.k.a. Danny "Sunshine" Bauer) is the host of the #1 downloaded podcast for school leaders, *Better Leaders Better Schools* (BLBS). Started in 2015, BLBS, was created out of a need for his own leadership development. Seeing that his district gathered leaders only to add more to their to-do lists without actually developing their leadership capacity, Daniel had an epiphany: "If I can have regular conversations with leaders who have more experience than me and implement what I learn from them, then I will become a better leader." In order to impact as many leaders as possible, Daniel recorded these conversations and made them available to the world, for free, via his podcast. He now hosts his second hit podcast, *The School Leadership Series*, which offers daily week-day inspiration to school administrators and educators in five minutes or less a day.

As "merely" a podcast host, Daniel pivoted in his career from leading at a local school to becoming a leader of leaders. His podcasts have impacted countless lives and because of the demand for his coaching, insights, and expertise, "The Mastermind," a world-class leadership community for educators, was born. His clients hail from multiple countries and continents around the world and they congregate weekly in virtual group coaching sessions. Daniel helps school administrators fight isolation and frustration through this leadership community in order to gain clarity and find solutions to their greatest challenges. There is a waiting list for this community, but interested school leaders can apply for admission at BetterLeadersBetterSchools.com/mm.

Readers are encouraged to reach out to Daniel to check his availability to speak to your organization concerning leadership, productivity, vision, culture, and systems. Connect with Daniel via @alienearbud all over social media, subscribe to his podcasts, and get his latest updates on his website, BetterLeadersBetterSchools.com.

LEARN MORE AT

BetterLeadersBetterSchools.com